HISTORY OF INDIA

HISTORY OF INDIA

Edited by
A. V. WILLIAMS JACKSON, Ph. D., LL.D.

VOLUME VII

The European Struggle for Indian Supremacy in the Seventeenth Century

BY

Sir William Wilson Hunter, K.C.S.I.
M.A., LL.D.

GYAN

Published by

GYAN

Gyan Publishing House
5, Ansari Road
Daryaganj, New Delhi-110002
Phone: 011-47034999, 9811692060
E-mail: books@gyanbooks.com

Distribution Network
gyanbooks.com
India, USA, Canada, UK, Australia, France

ISBN : 978-81-212-6772-4 (Set)
978-81-212-6766-3 (PB)
First Published, 1906

2nd Impression 2022

Printed at: Gyan Press, Delhi.

HISTORY OF INDIA (VOL. VII)
Author: Sir William Wilson Hunter

Malabar Hill, Bombay

Malabar Hill, a high ridge running out into the sea and overlooking Bombay, forms one of the favourite suburbs of the city. From the heights, on which there are many handsome houses, one obtains a magnificent view across the bay and over the city lying in the distance.

History of India

Edited by

A. V. WILLIAMS JACKSON, Ph. D., LL. D.
Professor of Indo-Iranian Languages in Columbia University

VOLUME VII

From the first European Settlements to the Founding of the English East India Company

By

SIR WILLIAM WILSON HUNTER, K. C. S. I., M. A., LL. D.
A Vice-President of the Royal Asiatic Society

INTRODUCTION BY THE EDITOR

The story of Indian events in the seventeenth century, so far as they relate to the internal history of the country during the time of the zenith and decline of the Moghul Empire, has already been told in the fourth and fifth volumes; what may be called the external history of India during this period is contained in the present volume and consists in a narrative of the struggle between the three rival European powers, Portuguese, Dutch, and English, for supremacy in Hindustan. The story is an involved one, but is remarkably clear and logical in its sequence.

The foothold established by the East India Company in 1600 was strengthened more and more by the separate voyages of the Company; and so vigorous was the advance made that it resulted in bringing England into conflict first with the Portuguese and afterwards with the Dutch as to which should have the upper hand in India. Bloodshed and international difficulties were the issue, but the ultimate outcome was the paramount establishment of English supremacy on the Bombay coast, the Madras coast, and the Bengal coast, forming the basis eventually of the three great organized presidencies of Hindustan and the absolute dominion of England which made India a part of the British Empire.

The narrative of the successive events by which all this was gradually accomplished forms one of the most instructive chapters in the world's history and is to be commended to the thoughtful reader.

A. V. WILLIAMS JACKSON.

CONTENTS

LIST OF ILLUSTRATIONS

WOOD AND IVORY MOSAIC IN THE GOLDEN TEMPLE AT AMRITSAR.

CHAPTER I

THE "SEPARATE VOYAGES" OF THE COMPANY

1601 - 1612

THE weakness in the constitution of the English East India Company made itself felt from the outset. Its capital proved insufficient for a single voyage; additional calls amounting to four shillings in the pound had to be levied from the subscribers and in some cases to be enforced by warrants of committal from the Privy Council. In the midst of these troubles the governor, Thomas Smythe, fell under suspicion of complicity in the Earl of Essex's rebellion, and was thrown into prison. The deputy-governor's health broke down under the strain of fitting out vessels and coercing defaulters, and an *ad interim* governor had to be suddenly chosen on April 11, 1601. Finally, however, the four ships,[1] which had dropped down from Woolwich in February, got fairly started from Torbay on April 22, 1601.

James Lancaster, the hero of the Cape voyage to India in 1591-1594, commanded the squadron, with a cargo of British staples, cloth, lead, tin, cutlery, glass, etc., worth £6860, and silver to the amount of £28,742. Arriving at Achin, in Sumatra, on June 5, 1602, he

WOOLWICH IN 1662.

delivered Queen Elizabeth's letter to the king, together with presents, received in return a treaty of amity, and was made welcome to the trade of the place. But unfortunately the pepper crop had failed in the preceding season, and Lancaster found that if his voyage was to be made a success, it must be by other methods than those of peaceful trade. The Company had, under the politic name of "reprisals," given him a strong hint "to take such course therein as he shall think meet" with regard to enemies of the realm. He interpreted this as a sanction to join the Dutch in an attack upon the "Portugals," still in a state of war with England, and captured a richly laden carrack of 900 tons. Hav-

[1] For details concerning the ships see Appendix II, B.

ing transferred her cargo to his own ships, he let the plundered Portuguese vessel go her way.

A good freight thus secured, Lancaster filled up his ships with spices at several of the islands, made a friend of the boy-king of Bantam, left a factory of English merchants and seamen, and returned to England on September 11, 1603. Two of his ships preceded him. On June 16th the Company had received the glad news that the *Ascension* was in the Thames, and forthwith ordered "six suits of canvas doublet and hose *without pockets*," for six porters to land her precious spices. The profits, apart from the plunder, were very large. The pepper had cost at Bantam, including dues, under 6*d*. per lb., while the selling price in England in 1599 had been raised from 3*s*. to 6*s*. and 8*s*. Its ordinary price was formerly 2*s*. 8*d*., and although it sank after the establishment of the Company to 2*s*. or even less, the returns were great. The gain on the finer spices was still larger. I find that £2948 paid in 1606 for cloves in Amboyna fetched £36,287 in London in 1608.

These enormous profits on Indian commodities, ranging from 500 to 1500 per cent., should at once have established the credit of the Company. But when the ships returned in 1603, the plague had brought business to a stand. Between December 7, 1602, and December 1, 1603, the Company declared that no fewer than 38,138 persons died of the pestilence in London; that all the merchants and people of condition had fled; and that "trade hath utterly ceased within the City for almost this half year." When the plague abated, difficulties arose in disposing of the cargoes for cash. The subscribers had to take part payment in pepper and sell it as best they might; nor was it until 1609 that the affairs of the first voyage of 1601 could be wound up and the profits finally distributed. They amounted to 95 per cent. on the subscription; a large return if it had been quickly realized. The ordinary rate of interest was then 8 per cent. per annum, and the 95 per cent. profits only yielded 9½ per cent. if calculated over the ten years from the subscription in 1600—not a tempting reward for a risky voyage and the long vexations of winding up. But part of the 95 per cent. had been distributed in previous years.

As a matter of fact, the Company seemed on the return of its first expedition in 1603 to be at its last gasp. It required at once to find £35,000 for seamen's wages and the king's dues; the plague had closed the market for its spices, and no money could be raised on loans. The Charter of 1600 authorized the sending forth of "six good ships and six good pinnaces at all times" during fifteen years, yet three years had passed and only four ships had sailed. Elizabeth seems to have expected a yearly expedition. In November, 1601, she notified her "mislike of the slackness of the Company," "propounding unto them the example of the Dutch, who do prosecute their voyages with a more honourable resolution." By 1603 the Privy Council lost patience at the prolonged delay, and the Company found itself compelled to project a second voyage.

The governor had in 1601 been directed to examine

the charter to see if power were given to compel members to contribute to a further venture. A second voyage was resolved on, and the book sent round by the beadle, but only the paltry sum of £11,000 was subscribed. The freemen declined even to attend the Gen-

QUEEN ELIZABETH.

eral Court to discuss the question, and had to be summoned afresh under "a pain of twenty shillings upon every one that maketh default." Finally, in 1603, when the pepper ships came home, "the Company resolved as a matter of necessity" that every subscriber of

£250 to the first voyage should advance another £200 for a second voyage. "In consideration of which he should receive pepper at a settled price to the amount of £500, which he should dispose of at his own discretion."

The four ships of the first voyage were taken over for the second, and sailed again from Gravesend in March, 1604, but with a cargo of only £1142 in goods. Its total freight, including specie, barely amounted to £12,302, as against the £28,602 sent out by the first voyage. Even this slender equipment was achieved only by making the profits of the first voyage responsible also for the second, so that practically the two ventures traded as a joint concern. Captain (afterwards Sir Henry) Middleton, in chief command of the squadron, loaded two ships with pepper at Bantam, where Lancaster had left a factory, and sent on the two others to Amboyna for the finer spices, particularly cloves. He returned to England in 1606, having lost the *Susan* on the voyage. The joint profits of this and of the first voyage yielded, as I have said, 95 per cent., but the final division could not be made till 1609.

These timid ventures contrasted with the magnificent operations of the Dutch Company, with its capital of £540,000 and its great yearly fleets. The English political economy of the day denounced the folly of sending forth the treasure of the realm; for the store of precious metals possessed by a country was then reckoned the measure of the nation's wealth. If we remember that the whole goods shipped by the first two voyages amounted to only £8002, and the coin or specie to no less than £32,902, we may understand how strong the argument appeared. Gerard de Malynes laid his finger on this "canker of the commonwealth." He compared our export of bullion for spices to "the simplicity of the West Indians" "in giving the good commodities of their countries, yea gold, silver, and precious

SIGNATURE OF QUEEN ELIZABETH.
(Harleian Ms. No. 285.)

things for beads, bells, knives, looking-glasses, and such toys and trifles."

While the political economists condemned the nature of the trade, the Crown grew more and more dissatisfied with its petty results. The East India Company, like the Levant and Muscovy Companies, had weathered the storm of popular indignation which led Elizabeth in 1601 to abolish most of the monopolies; as so distant a trade manifestly demanded a strong corporate body vested with exclusive rights. But the accession of James I opened the door to more subtle influences, and an expelled member of the Company, who was also a courtier, worked them for his own ends. Sir Edward Michelborne, a soldier-adventurer of good family in the reign of Elizabeth, appears among the patentees named in her charter to the Company in December, 1600, but he does not seem to have actually put money into the concern. He had, however, procured a letter from the Lord Treasurer to the committees in 1600, recommending his appointment "as a principal commander" on the expedition. This the Company evaded on the ground that "they purpose not to employ any gentleman in any place of charge or commandment in the said voyage," lest "the generality" should "withdraw their contributions." In the following year, 1601, Michelborne was disfranchised by the Company on the ground that he had not paid up his subscription to the first voyage.

Having been implicated in the Essex rebellion, he had to digest his wrath as best he could during the remaining years of Elizabeth. But the accession of James gave him his opportunity, and in June, 1604, he obtained a royal license of discovery and trade from Cambay on the coast of India to China, "notwithstanding any grant or charter to the contrary." The reduced scale of the Company's second voyage which had lately sailed gave colour to this infringement of its privileges, and the new grant was confined to traffic at places where the Company had not established itself. But Michelborne's ideas of "trade and discovery" were founded on the buccaneering models of Elizabeth's reign. After eighteen months of piracy, during which he attacked the Dutch at Bantam, plundered a Chinese ship, and made the English name abhorred in the Eastern seas, he returned to England in 1606, never to sail again.

This first of the "Interlopers" had seriously compromised the position of the Company in the Archipelago. "If there should any more such as he be permitted by His Majesty to come into these parts," wrote its factor at Bantam, "our estate here would be very dangerous." King James had put an end to the nineteen years' state of war with Spain and Portugal by the treaty of 1604, and although the hostility between the nations in the East still smouldered, our captains could no longer obtain a cargo by rifling a Portuguese ship, as Captain Lancaster boldly did on the first voyage. While the Company had thus lost an enfeebled prey, it had made a powerful enemy. The Dutch were stronger in the East than the Portuguese and the English put together, and for Michelborne's attack on them a heavy price was to be paid. Their reprisals for Bantam ended in the tragedy of Amboyna.

The Company's third expedition, consisting of three vessels under Captain Keeling, Captain Hawkins, and Captain David Middleton, sailed in 1607, and brought home a rich cargo of pepper from Bantam and cloves from Amboyna, which, together with the profits of plunder, yielded 234 per cent. on the subscriptions. Before its tardy return the Company had almost lost heart. For on the arrival of the ships from the second voyage, in 1606, the difficulties of realizing the profit seemed so great that "most of the Members were inclined to wind up their affairs and drop the business."

They were stirred into fresh action partly by royal promises and partly by a new royal menace to their privileges—the grant to Richard Penkevell to trade to China and the Spice Islands by way of the northwest or northeast passage. No real harm came to the Company this time; but it felt compelled to fit out a fourth

WILLIAM HAWKINS.

voyage in 1608. It could raise only a capital of less than half that subscribed for the first voyage, and barely sufficient to equip two ships, both of which perished at sea. The contributors lost their money, and in 1609 only one ship could be sent out on the fifth voyage, with a capital of less than a fifth of the subscription to the first voyage in 1601.

This proved the low-water mark in the Company's fortunes. The fifth voyage in 1609 was practically equipped by the subscribers to the third voyage, and the good management of the two left a profit of 234 per cent. on the joint venture. King James also began to interest himself in his new subjects' enterprise beyond the seas. In 1609 he followed up an earlier grant by finally founding Virginia, the first great English colony, and he issued a new and more ample charter to the East India Company, securing to it "the whole, entire, and only trade" into "the East Indies." Any persons not licensed by the Company who "directly or indirectly do visit, haunt, frequent, or trade," "into or from any of the said East Indies," were to incur the royal "indignation" and the forfeiture of their ships and goods, half to the Company and half to the Crown. James closely adhered to the terms and even to the words of Elizabeth, but where a divergence occurred it tended to strengthen the Company. Thus the new Charter of 1609 was to be in perpetuity and not for fifteen years, like Elizabeth's. In case the grant did not prove profitable to the realm, a notice of three years, instead of two, was to be given by the Crown.

The East India Company now began to be the fashion. Elizabeth's Charter of 1600 was granted to the privateering Earl of Cumberland and 217 commoners, chiefly City men. The list in King James's Charter of 1609 is headed by a powerful band of courtiers. It is addressed to "Our right trusty and right well-beloved Cousins and Councellors, Robert Earl of Salisbury, Our

High Treasurer of England, Charles Earl of Nottingham, Our High Admiral of England, and Edward Earl of Worcester, Master of Our Horse, and Our Right Trusty and Well-beloved William Lord Cavendish, and Our Well-beloved Servant Sir Thomas Lake, Knight, One of the Clerks of Our Signet," and other knights and gentlemen. Royal favouritism had become a power in the State, and it was highly convenient that the Earl of Salisbury, who stands first in the list of adventurers, should also have the control of the export of treasure from the realm and of his Majesty's customs. Men of rank sought the freedom of the corporation, and in July, 1609, the Earl of Southampton sent a brace of bucks to the Brethren " to make merry withal in regard of their kindness in accepting him of their Company." A venison committee was promptly chosen, " who agree upon a dinner to be provided for the whole company at the Governor's house."

Under these happier auspices the unprecedented subscription of £82,000 was raised for the sixth voyage of 1610, commanded by Sir Henry Middleton. Elaborate instructions were given for the conduct of its business, for the prevention of private trading by the Company's captains or factors, and as to the commodities to be purchased in the East—raw silk, fine book-calicoes, indigo, cloves, and mace. The Company had in 1607 decided to build ships for themselves at their hired dock at Deptford, and they now took up this business on a great scale. In 1609 they launched a leviathan of 1100 tons—the *Trades Increase*. The King himself consented to name the ship, and came down to the docks accompanied by the queen, the prince, and the court, for the ceremony. The Company entertained him at " a great banquet, all served on dishes and plates of china-ware [then a rarity more prized than silver plate], and his Majesty placed a great chain of gold and a medal about Sir Thomas Smythe's [the Governor's] neck with his own hands." The *Trades Increase*—" for beauty, burthen, strength, and sufficiency," says a contemporary writer, " surpassing all merchants' ships whatsoever "—proved, notwithstanding her royal sponsorship, an unlucky craft. After a brief career, while careening at Bantam, she was burned by the natives. Her brave captain, Sir Henry Middleton, died there soon afterwards, in 1613, it is said of grief.

The next two voyages, in 1611 and 1612, were also on a large scale. Events had occurred in the East which rendered the English system of small separate adventures extremely hazardous. In 1609 the Dutch closed their long war with Spain by a truce for twelve years, and had no longer any cause for keeping well with the English in Asiatic waters. By this truce, ill observed as it was in the East, the Portuguese were also left more free to deal with the English intruders. About the same time our ships came into conflict with the Asiatic land powers. Sir Henry Middleton, commanding the sixth voyage (1610), was seized and imprisoned, together with many of his people, by the Governor of Mocha, on the Red Sea. Captain Hawkins also found opposition at the court of the Indian emperor, whither he had gone to arrange for a permanent factory at Surat.

Complications were thus arising on land and sea with which the English system of " Separate Voyages " was manifestly unable to cope. Not only therefore were the voyages of 1611 and 1612 on a large scale, but a new element of combination also entered into their equipment. The separate subscribers of the previous six voyages of the Company became the " joint adventurers " of the seventh in 1611. The following year they united so closely that the eighth voyage in 1612 was sometimes reckoned the First Joint Stock.

A BANYAN, OR NATIVE MERCHANT OF SURAT.

I now summarize in tabular form the operations of the Company during its first twelve years of Separate Voyages. The following figures are extracted from a statement prepared about 1620 and reproduced in the India Office folio of " Marine Records." They agree with the list of voyages given by the Company's historiographer, from whose " Annals " I compile the column of profits.[1] But as the concluding ones were more or less joint undertakings with distinct branches, the number of separate expeditions is variously reckoned from nine to twelve. Thus the so-called " tenth " which fought Best's famous fight off Suwali is included by the Company's historiographer and in the Marine Records' list under the eighth: as also the " eleventh," which consisted of one ship detached from it. The " twelfth " was likewise a single-ship expedition, commissioned chiefly to carry back the Persian ambassador.

The difference in enumeration does not affect the main results. Macpherson, who takes the number of Separate Voyages at twelve, from 1601 to 1612-1613, gives the total capital employed at £464,284. My table, which takes the number at nine, shows an aggregate capital of £466,179.

The column of profits may awaken the envy of modern merchants. But they represent the gains both on the exports and the imports of the voyage, together with the results of " cabotage," or port-to-port barter, during the long stay of the ships in the East. On the return of each expedition, money had to be found at once to pay off the crews, and within a certain period for the king's customs. But the cargo could sometimes not be sold until the royal share of the pepper had been disposed of, and then only at long credits of eighteen months to two years. In many cases the subscribers had to take payment for their contributions in spices or calicoes and to find a purchaser for them as best

[1] These statistics are given in Appendix II, C.

they could. The system of "candle-auctions," by public notice hung up at the Royal Exchange, afterwards relieved them of this burden. According to that system, the Company offered the commodities brought home by the ships at its London mart, with an inch of lighted candle on the desk. As long as the candle burned, fresh offers could be received, and the goods were knocked down to the highest bidder before the wick guttered out. At such auctions, even before 1622, a hundred thousand pounds' worth of silk, indigo, or spices was sometimes disposed of in a single parcel.

The candle-auction became the regular method for the East India Company's sales. Before it opened, "a black list" of defaulters or others who had wronged the Brethren was read out, and the persons thus named were not allowed "to bid at the candle." At one sale in 1667 over four hundred lots were disposed of, and the carpenter's bill "for setting up and taking down the scaffolds in the Great Hall" shows that the auctions were attended with some ceremony. But the government preferred to deal more privately with the Company. Thus in 1669, when the Lords Commissioners of his Majesty's Ordnance wanted four hundred pounds of saltpetre, they declared "it was not honourable nor decent for the King to buy at the candle as other common persons did . . . and therefore insisted to buy it by contract."

Before this system fully developed, the divided interests arising out of the Separate Voyages led to a delay of six or eight years before the accounts of each expedition could be rendered. A non-official estimate gives the net profit at under twenty per cent. per annum on the capital invested: which "would perhaps be reduced to a level with the common interest of the time, if the expense of insurance were deducted." Without accepting this calculation, it is certain that under the Charter of Elizabeth (1600 - 1609) the Company found great difficulty in raising capital for each successive voyage. They made frequent appeals to patriotic sentiment, declaring their adventure to be a "public action" "for the honour of our native country and for the advancement of trade," and "rather for the good of the Commonwealth of their country than for their private benefit."

The earlier voyages had been directed toward the Indian Archipelago, where the English trade had to be done either at islands in possession of the Portuguese, or at native ports in competition with the Dutch. King James's peace with Spain in 1604 technically shut out the Company from the Portuguese islands except with the consent of Portugal. For Elizabeth's Charter of 1600 had expressly precluded resort to any place or kingdom "in the lawful and actual possession" of any Christian prince who already or "hereafter shall be in league or amity with us, our heirs or successors, and who doth not or will not accept of such trade." This proviso was again inserted in King James's Charter of 1609, and although European treaties had little effect beyond the Cape of Good Hope, the king's project of the Spanish marriage made him anxious to avoid grounds of umbrage to the united Spanish and Portuguese crown.

While the English thus found their trade at his Catholic Majesty's settlements rendered dependent on the good-will of their Portuguese rivals, they began to encounter a keen competition at the Dutch marts

AN OLD PICTURE OF THE CAPE OF GOOD HOPE.

in the Archipelago. As early as 1603 that competition was felt by the Company in European prices, and it soon complicated the relations of the Dutch and English in the East. Michelborne's attack on the Dutch in 1605 was defended, and by many Englishmen condoned, on the plea of " the insolences of the Hollanders." The commander of the Company's fourth voyage (1608) was reduced by the Dutch intrigues at Achin to barter his cargo with ships from Gujarat. The fifth voyage under Captain David Middleton met with still stronger opposition after 1609. The Dutch truce with Spain in that year removed the need of any further complaisance to the English. Within ten years after the grant of Elizabeth's Charter, the English found their old Portuguese prey in the Archipelago placed by treaty beyond their grasp, and their old Dutch allies no longer in want of their help, and turned into bitter trade rivals.

The simple remedy, as it now appears to us, would have been to withdraw from the contest for the produce of the islands, and to open up a direct traffic with the Asiatic continent. But the simple method is not always the obvious one. The tradition of Eastern commerce was that India yielded only the cheaper spices, pepper, and ginger, and furnished ports for trans-shipment of the more precious ones of the farther East—mace, cinnamon, and cloves. To shift our factories from the Archipelago to India seemed at the time equivalent to giving up the direct trade in the most lucrative commodities, and sinking into middlemen like the early Arab merchants on the Malabar coast.

Nevertheless the English soon began to feel their way toward India itself. The mission of Mildenhall (or Midnall), sent forth by Staper and armed with a letter from Queen Elizabeth in 1599 to the Great Moghul, returned in 1602 with news of the high civilization and boundless resources of the Indian court. Captain Hawkins, of the third voyage (1607), proceeded to the Indian coast with a letter from James I to the Emperor

Jahangir, and obtained permission to establish a factory at Surat. But in spite of Hawkins giving a pledge of loyalty to the emperor by marrying "a white mayden out of his palace," the Portuguese succeeded in getting the grant revoked, and Hawkins, after two and a half years of fruitless negotiation at the court of Agra, left in disgust. In 1609 the English obtained an unstable footing at Surat, and their letters begin to appear in the records of the Company. On August 30, 1609, one of them sent home an exhaustive price-list of Indian goods and of English commodities vendible at that port.

A main object of the sixth voyage of 1610 under Sir Henry Middleton was to establish a trade with the Red Sea. But Middleton's reprisals after his seizure by the Governor of Mocha stirred up the Moslem zeal against the English, and placed us in an awkward position with the Moghul emperor. Sir Henry's attempt to trade at Surat in 1611 was frustrated by a Portuguese fleet, which barred his entrance to the river, and by the ill-will of the Mussulman governor, so that he was forced back upon the old marts in the Eastern Archipelago.

Another expedition (1611), under the direction of two merchants who had been in the Dutch service, was intended to open up a trade between India and the Spice Islands. It sailed for Pulicat, the chief port of Southeastern India, and coasted up the Bay of Bengal as far as Masulipatam, north of Madras, buying calicoes which it carried for sale to Bantam and Siam. In 1611-1612 Captain Saris, commanding the *Clove*, was provided with a pass from the Turkish emperor, ordering his governors on the Red Sea to admit the English to friendly trade. But the Moslem ill-will, left behind by Sir Henry Middleton's "rummaging of Indian ships," rendered a traffic on shore impracticable. After a barter of cargoes enforced on Moslem vessels at sea, and something like a compact of piracy with Middle-

A GENERAL VIEW OF MASULIPATAM.

ton, Captain Saris proceeded to Japan, which he reached on June 12, 1613.

There he found a solitary Englishman, whose story savours of the time. William Adams, having served as master in Elizabeth's navy and in the English Company of Barbary Merchants, joined a Dutch fleet from Rotterdam to the East Indies as pilot-major in 1598. After long miseries the fleet got scattered, but Adams's ship reached Japan in April, 1600, with the crew in a dying state. Adams was brought before the emperor, examined as to his country and the cause of his coming, and then thrown into prison for six weeks. The Portuguese tried to get him put to death, but eventually he rose by ship-building into favour with the emperor, and received an estate " like unto a lordship in England."

In 1609 the Dutch obtained leave to establish a factory at the port of Firando, in Japan, and two years later a Dutch captain received through Adams's influence ample privileges of trade. Adams then learned for the first time that the English also had penetrated into the Eastern seas. In 1611 he wrote a letter, full of sturdy pathos, to his " unknown friends and countrymen," giving an account of his adventures and of the trade capabilities of Japan. On the arrival of Captain Saris in 1613, Adams secured permission from the emperor for an English factory, which was accordingly established, with the hopes of also opening out trade with Corea and China. Adams entered the Company's service on a salary of £100 a year, and made many voyages, although the project of a northeast passage, to which he, like many bold sailors of the day, looked forward, remained a dream.

The emperor liked him so well as to prevent his return to his wife and child in England, and in due time Adams provided himself with a wife and two children in Japan. He died in 1620, after seeing a persecution of the Christians by a new emperor, and left his estate impartially to his English and Japanese families. A road in Yedo was named Pilot Street in his honour, and a native festival still annually com-

THE PANCH MAHAL AT THE MOGHUL COURT AT FATHPUR - SIKRI.

memorates the first Englishman who lived and died in Japan.

Wherever the English had gone they had encountered the hostility of the Portuguese. It was not alone in the Moluccas and Philippines, where Portugal had rights based on actual possession of certain of the islands. But in the great empires of India and Japan also, where all Europeans were but humble strangers, the Portuguese determined that for the English there should be no thoroughfare. In Japan they would have had Adams executed; they plotted with the native governors against our settling on the Indian coast; they procured the revocation of the grant to Hawkins at the court of the Great Moghul. The treaty of 1604 tied the hands of our captains, and if James I had one eye to his subjects' interests, he had the other to a family alliance with Spain.

Fortunately the Portuguese themselves brought about a collision. Their fleet had prevented our ships from landing at Surat in 1611, and had compelled them to do what business they could by exchanging cargoes at sea. In 1612 Captain Thomas Best, with the *Red Dragon* and a smaller vessel, the *Hosiander*, arrived off Suwali, at the mouth of the Surat or Tapti River, with orders from the Company to conciliate the goodwill of the Indian emperor for trade on that coast. On November 29th four Portuguese ships, mounting over 120 guns, attended by twenty-six or thirty "frigates," or rowed galleys for boarding, appeared off Suwali, with the intent to capture the two English vessels. Best saw that the Portuguese admiral and vice-admiral were separated by the tide and shoals from the rest. He promptly bore down on the two great ships in the *Red Dragon*, but the *Hosiander* could not get clear of her anchors, and the single English ship had to fight the desperate battle alone. He steered straight at the enemy, calmly reserving his fire till he got between the admiral and vice-admiral, and then delivered such a cannonade on either side that "by an hour we had well peppered" them "with some 56 great shot."

The *Red Dragon* had her mainmast struck and her longboat sunk by cannon-balls, but she anchored in sight of the Portuguese for the night. Early next morning (November 30th) Best again steered into the enemy, now accompanied by the *Hosiander*, which had got clear of her anchors and "bravely redeemed the former day's doing nothing." The mouth of the Surat estuary was then encumbered (as it is now closed for ships) by silt banks, and rendered dangerous by strong currents. The silt of the Tapti River, near whose mouth Surat lay, together with the deposits from the obstructed sea currents, had formed a long shoal dry at high water, along the coast. Inside this shoal lay the Suwali anchorage, seven miles long by one and one-half miles broad, with sandspits and bars on the shore side—an ideal battle-ground for the skilful handling of the English ships against the superior numbers of the heavy Portuguese.

Three of the galleons were driven on the sands, the

Hosiander keeping up a fierce fire, "and danced the hay about them so that they durst not show a man upon the hatches." At 9 A. M. the English captain, probably fearing to go aground himself with an ebb-tide on the shallows, stood out into deeper water and anchored. The respite enabled the Portuguese frigates to come to the aid of the three galleons, which they

AN EARLY TYPE OF ENGLISH SHIP.

"shoared up with their yards," and so got afloat again. In the afternoon, as soon as the tide permitted, the English renewed the fight, and kept it up till dark, when they anchored in the estuary six miles from the Portuguese. At 9 P. M. the enemy sent a fire-ship down upon the *Hosiander*, but the English sank her by a cannonade, with an estimated loss to the Portuguese of between 120 and 140 men.

Next day, December 1 (1612), passed without fighting, the wearied combatants riding at anchor. On the 2d, Best sailed twenty miles along the coast, hoping the enemy would follow, but they declined. Their rowed "frigates," which were helpful to them and annoying to us among the shoals and currents of the estuary, would have been easily disposed of by our ships in the open sea and with a steady breeze. Best anchored in the neighbouring bay of Moha, whence he aided the Moghul troops in besieging a pirate fort. On December 22d the Portuguese squadron, including the four great galleons, having reinforced itself at Diu, again hove in sight. At daybreak on the 23d Best boldly attacked against overwhelming odds, and kept up the fight till ten or eleven o'clock, or, as some say, till two in the afternoon. The Indian soldiers crowded down to the beach to watch our two ships battling with a whole armada. The fight ended in the complete rout of the enemy, and Best chased the flying squadron for four hours.

It seemed, however, impossible that the enormous force of the Portuguese ships should not in the end prevail. But on December 24 (1612) a final engagement was fought. The Portuguese were decisively put to flight. We were, however, so exhausted that the pursuit could not be pressed, and on the 27th Best's two ships triumphantly reopened communication with our factors at Surat. During the month's fighting the enemy lost 160 men according to their own account, or three hundred to five hundred according to English

Hookah Smokers in India

Smoking is almost as common in India as it is throughout the rest of the world, and although the Moghul Emperor Jahangir, in the sixteenth century, like King James, issued a counterblast against tobacco, the Hindu, the Moslem, and even occasionally the Parsi, enjoys his "hookah" or "hubble-bubble," or, if he can afford it, his briar-wood pipe and cigar.

estimates. Best lost only three, and the stout old *Red Dragon*, not a new ship when bought from the Earl of Cumberland in 1600, had still six years of good service before her. Her end came in 1619, when she and two other English vesels were taken off Sumatra by six Dutch ships after a desperate fight. The Hollanders offered to restore her, but the English declined, as her captors "had lamed her with misusage." The gallant Thomas Best rose to the height of his profession. He appears as late as 1637 as Master of Trinity House, and in 1638 on a commission to inquire into frauds in the supply of timber.

The severest combat took place before the eyes of the Moghul troops, "all the camp standing by the seaside looking on us." This running-fight of a single month broke the reputation which the Portuguese had won in India by the sea achievements of a hundred years. As a land-power they had sunk into insignificance on the establishment of the Moghul Empire in Southern India during the second half of the preceding century. The coast governors of that empire now turned with the tide in favour of the English, and Best found it easy to obtain sanction for a factory at Surat and at three other places around the Gulf of Cambay. By a formal instrument all grievances arising out of Sir Henry Middleton's reprisals were buried in oblivion; our merchandise was to be subject only to a moderate fixed duty of 3½ per cent.; and in event of the death of the English factors, the Company's property was to be kept safe by the Indian authorities for delivery to our next fleet. This agreement with the Governor of Surat, in December, 1612, was duly ratified by an imperial *Farmān*, or decree, delivered with Oriental pomp to Captain Best at Suwali in January, 1613.

From this imperial decree our legal settlement on the Indian continent dates. It marks a new departure

VIEW OF CAMBAY FROM THE SOUTH IN 1772.

in the history of the English Company—a new departure which was to end in our withdrawal from the Archipelago and our establishment in India. In the same year (1612 - 1613) the Company at home developed its system of separate voyages into what was known as the system of Joint Stock. By this change it sought to increase its strength so as to join on more equal terms in the contest of the European nations for the Spice Islands. But in its settlement at Surat it had unconsciously provided a retreat for itself to a wider sphere of action, when worsted in that struggle.

CHAPTER II

THE STRUGGLE WITH THE PORTUGUESE

1612 - 1622

CAPTAIN BEST'S fight off Suwali in 1612 sounded like a trumpet-call to the nation. It found the Company ready to make a gallant response. Having resolved in 1612 to adopt the Joint Stock system, the committees raised an unprecedented subscription of £429,000 in 1613—about equal to the total of all the separate ventures since 1600. They thus got command of a capital which might almost vie with that of the Dutch Company, or with the state-resources of Portugal. The whole sum was not, however, called up at once, but was to be paid during four years for an annual voyage, so that the actual number of ships employed still remained insignificant compared with the long established fleets of England's rivals.

Before entering on the political events which grew out of this development, let me briefly summarize its commercial results. The four voyages extended from 1613 to 1616, with an average capital of £107,000; a fleet of about seven ships a year which exported goods and silver averaging £47,379 on each voyage, and yielded an average profit of 87½ per cent. on the aggregate capital employed.[1] The return would have been much larger but for the hostility of the Dutch and Portuguese. The two voyages of 1613-1614 are said to have yielded a profit of 120 per cent., and one cargo bought for £9000 in the East sold for £80,000 in England.

By the beginning of 1614 what is officially reckoned as "the voyage of 1613" was ready. It consisted of four vessels; the flagship having been launched on January 1st under the name of the *New Year's Gift*, 550 tons—armed and strongly built for trade or war. The command-in-chief was given to a captain of proved capacity for both. Nicholas Downton had been "Lieutenant-General," or second in command, under Sir Henry Middleton in the sixth voyage of 1610, which came to blows with the Turks in the Red Sea, and left a record of reprisals not soon forgotten by the Moslem world. After many adventures and long trading in the East, Downton brought home his ship, the *Peppercorn*, with her timbers strained and gaping, in the autumn of 1613, most of his crew dead, the remainder rotting with scurvy, he himself stricken by disease, and his half-sinking craft with difficulty making the Downs. His unconquerable endurance won for him the command of the great expedition then being fitted out, and in March, 1614, he sailed as "General" of the first Joint Stock voyage.

He carried with him the amplest powers which the Company could desire or the Crown grant. For the

[1] For statistics concerning the four voyages see Appendix II, D.

discipline of his fleet, King James vested in him full power to execute the cruel chastisements then "commonly used in all armies at sea," with martial law for the punishment by death of mutiny or other capital offences. As regards foreign rivals, his Majesty gave

KING JAMES I.

much good advice mingled with some useful suggestions.

"For as much as at this present," he declared, "We are in amity with all Christian princes," "And because We are not ignorant of the emulation and envy which doth accompany the discovery of countries and trade, and of the quarrels and contentions which do many times fall out between the subjects of diverse princes when they meet the one with the other in foreign and far remote countries in prosecuting the course of their discoveries," We charge you, Nicholas Downton, not to " go about to set upon " any of our Christian allies, especially Spain, " except you shall be by them first thereunto justly provoked." If, however, this should happen, " you shall not for any act or acts " needful in the case, " be in danger or subject to the peril and penalties of our laws." Above all you are " to suffer no spoil to be made of any goods or merchandise " which " shall be recovered by you," " but to see them safely brought home with their bills of lading, so that We may adjust matters hereafter," with the offending State.

Truly an Elizabethan commission drafted with an eye to making out an *ex post facto* diplomatic case worthy of the Great Queen, yet, in spite of its Jacobean pedantry, disclosing a clear perception of the realities of distant sea-trade. James recognized that European treaties had little effect beyond the Cape of Good Hope. He desired his subjects to abstain from offence, yet if offences must needs come, not to be the losers by them; and to repel force by force.

Captain Downton thoroughly grasped the situation. Should spoliation be going, he was determined not to be the despoiled. The fundamental difference of view taken by England and by Portugal as to their relative positions in the East inevitably led to conflict. From the moment that Da Gama's ships returned in 1499 the Portuguese dynasty affirmed its right to " the sovereignty and dominion of all we have discovered," besides its wider claim under the Demarcation Bull of

1493 and the treaties based upon it. From the first Charter of Elizabeth to the London Company in 1600 the English Crown acknowledged only Portuguese rights based on "actual possession," and altogether ignored the wider claim under the Demarcation Bull. But the "discovery" of continents and of groups of islands scattered over great oceans and the "actual possession" of them were widely different terms. The real question was—which of the two nations could enforce its view.

Ten years, from Best's coast fight in 1612 to our capture of Ormuz in 1622, sufficed to decide this issue. The Portuguese were no longer the gallant little nation, in the first heat of independence, which opened the Cape route to India and made themselves masters of the Asiatic seas. In less than two centuries from 1385, when the field of Aljubarrota had freed Portugal from the standing menace of Castile and launched her on a career of glory under the House of Aviz, that patriotic dynasty flickered out, and the Portuguese passed under the bigot rule of Philip II. The first half of their "sixty years' captivity" to Spain (1580 - 1640) sufficed to exhaust their resources in Philip's struggle with Dutch Protestantism, and to blight their national vigour.

Portugal ceased to be prolific of great men. The four successors of Albuquerque who stand out in Indian history belonged to the period before her "captivity" to Spain. Nuno da Cunha (1529 - 1538), who opened out the Portuguese trade to Bengal; João de

Castro (1545-1548), who defended the Portuguese possessions on the western coast from Diu down to Goa against the native powers, and strove to cleanse the Augean stable of Indo-Portuguese misrule; Constantino de Braganza (1558-1561), who conquered Daman and took up De Castro's task of internal reform; Luis de Athaide, viceroy from 1568 to 1571 and again from 1578 to 1581, who stemmed for a time the rising tide of revolt against Portuguese oppression and beat back the Moslem coalition in India and the Archipelago—were the products of an independent Portugal. Her forced union with Spain (1580-1640) was barren of heroes.

In India also a great political change had taken place. Although Portugal had more than held her own in the scuffle of the petty coast rajas, she had never made an impression even on the small isolated kingdoms of the inland south; and after the extension of the Moghul Empire southwards she ceased to have any significance as an Indian land-power.

In the height of her naval supremacy she had felt her weakness on shore. "We sit still," wrote one of her ablest servants, "perishing without lands out of which to support ourselves, or find shelter." The little patches of Indian coast did not afford a land-revenue sufficient to support the administration in peace or to serve as a security for loans in war. In 1546, the chivalrous viceroy, Dom João de Castro, having to raise a loan for the defence of Diu, ordered the body of his son, lately slain by the Moslems, to be exhumed, and given as a pledge for repayment. But the corpse had

BANGALORE, A TOWN IN SOUTHERN INDIA.

decayed. "Thus," he concludes, "having nothing left in this world, neither gold, silver, nor any other property except the beard on my face, I send it to you to remain with you as a gage."

As the "confusion of evils" reached its height in their coast-settlements, the Indo-Portuguese, now degenerated into colonies of half-breeds, tried to wring a living from sea-plunder. Their naval system had from the first lent itself to piracy and corsair descents. It developed into unrestrained buccaneering. The Portuguese caravels and galleys became the scourge of the Eastern routes. From their pirate nests on the Bay of Bengal they swooped down on the approaches to the Ganges and terrorized the rich coast traffic of Arrakan and Burma. Sometimes a successful adventurer like Nicote founded for himself a brief dominion. But hasty pillage, careless of the slaughter of infidels, was their main object. Gradually the Eastern sea-races from the Spice Islands to the Persian Gulf roused themselves against the Christian robbers. Ternate in the far Moluccas shook off the Portuguese yoke (1575-1576); Malacca, their great half-way place of strength, was again and again attacked by the King of Achin. Ceylon rose against them. Their Indian piracies brought on them the vengeance of the coast princes, and at length the crushing wrath of the Moghul Empire.

Wherever we turn we see the same spectacle of oppression and ruin. The Sular islanders of the most eastern archipelago would not on our first arrival come near our ships, as the Portuguese "had used to take them and make slaves of them." At the western extremity of the Asiatic trade-route the Shah of Persia sent an ambassador to Paris begging the King of France for help "to drive the Portuguese out of the East Indies."

But it was not the piracies of the Portuguese that most deeply stirred the much-enduring Eastern races. In 1320, Marino Sanuto the elder had submitted his famous *Secretum Fidelium Crucis* to the Pope, for seizing the Egyptian route and securing the proceeds of the Indian trade as a war fund to retake Jerusalem. To the Portuguese sovereigns and Grand Masters of the Military Order of Christ the conquest of the Asiatic Ocean seemed the true continuation of the Crusades. Their determined efforts to reach the Christian kingdom of Prester John, by land or by sea, ended in Da Gama's discovery of India. Seekers are apt to find what they go in quest of, and Da Gama's companions were at least half-convinced that the Malabar temples were Christian churches. On their return, King Emmanuel at once wrote to their Catholic Majesties that when these "Christian people" of India "shall have been fortified in the faith," they would help in "destroying the Moors of those parts." To Rome he announced that "the king [of Calicut] looks upon himself and the major part of his people as Christian." This exaggeration, although quickly corrected, served to perpetuate the legend of the Crusades.

The Portuguese in fact, by a happy chance, landed on a strip of Indian coast to which the ancient trade-route had brought Nestorian emigrants, and where Christians had long formed a recognized caste. But the zeal of the newcomers could not rest satisfied with their good fortune. They resolved to turn the old "St. Thomas" Christians into Catholics, and the infidels who came under their power they strove, by force or

A MONOLITHIC TEMPLE AT MAHABALIPUR IN SOUTHERN INDIA.

threats, to convert. The appalling narrative of their cruelty and folly forms part of the general history of Christianity in India, but need not be entered into here. The early intermittent methods of the friars, who arrived with the annual fleets, blossomed into a native church under the apostolic teaching of St. Francis Xavier (1542) and the Society of Jesus. But the saintly fervour of the great Jesuit proved too mild for the Dominican bigots who, in the complaint of the Goanese, " cast souls into hell through fear." In 1560 the Inquisition was established in India under the Dominican Order. Its atrocities reached Europe in a perhaps exaggerated form. But a Portuguese writer states that seventy-one *autos da fé*, or general burnings, were held in 173 years, and that at " a few " of them 4046 persons were sentenced to various punishments, 121 being condemned to the flames.

These savageries were perpetrated chiefly, but not altogether, on the unhappy Nestorian or " St. Thomas " Christians, who had dwelt quietly in India for centuries before the advent of the Portuguese. Wherever the Portuguese established their power, from Ceylon to the distant Spice Islands, they tried to make conversions. Every convert was a possible apostate, and to apostasy the Inquisition showed no mercy. The tolerant spirit which I have noticed in some of the early Portuguese treaties with native princes seemed little short of a denial of Christ to the zealot who in 1580 united the crowns of Portugal and Spain. Philip II would have no paltering with either the Indian infidels or the orthodox Nestorians. After drawing the rope tighter round the neck of Indian heresy in 1594, he delivered his stroke at the non-Christians in 1598. He learned that previous viceroys had granted some tolerant provisions in regard to the temples and worship of the native faiths. "I deem it good," wrote his Majesty, "that they be revised by the Inquisitors and theologians who reside in those parts."

In the following year, 1599, he struck a more fatal

blow at the ancient native Christians. The Synod of Diamper (*i.e.* Udayampura), assembled in session, then denounced Nestorius and his heresies, and for a time extinguished the Indian Nestorian Church. The sacred books of the "St. Thomas" congregations, their missals and church ornaments, were publicly burned, and their consecrated oil was poured upon the flames. Their religious nationality as a separate caste was abolished, and for the next half-century the Malabar Christians chafed under a line of Roman Catholic prelates, and groaned beneath the Inquisition. In the same year, 1599, in which the Synod of Diamper crushed the ancient Church of Malabar, the London merchants met in Founders' Hall to establish an East India Company.

DOM FR. ALEIXO DE MENEZES, THIRD ARCHBISHOP OF GOA AND FIRST PRIMATE OF THE EAST INDIES (1595-1610).

Portugal thus entered on her struggle with England for the Eastern seas burdened with the traditions of the past and beset by the passionate vengeance which her attempt to enforce those traditions had aroused among the Asiatic races. She represented the reactionary spirit of mediævalism, as against the modern methods of the Protestant nations. To the English and the Dutch, the Indies were simply a new world for commerce, to the Portuguese they were a vast arena for mingled commerce and crusades. The Indian trade of Portugal had dwindled since her union with Spain in 1580. Philip II wanted money for his wars. America supplied silver, the East Indies drained it away, and Philip could not any more than Charles V pay his troops in pepper and cloves.

The Spanish king had guaranteed in 1580 the undisturbed enjoyment of the East Indian trade to the Portuguese, and he kept his word by neglecting their Indian possessions. His heavy war demands dried up the Portuguese supplies of money and men; and the capital which the Jews formerly furnished had been driven by persecution to Holland. Of the 806 vessels which Portugal sent to India, from the setting forth of Vasco da Gama in 1497 to the English sea victory off Surat in 1612, only 186 sailed during the thirty-two years after the union of the two Iberian crowns in 1580. But the deterioration was in quality as well as in numbers. For of the sixty-six carracks or ships lost between 1497 and 1612, no fewer than thirty-five perished at sea during the thirty-two years of Spanish domination, besides four taken by the enemy. In 1596 Spain became bankrupt and repudiated her public debts. In 1612 the English ambassador reported from Madrid that "the Indian ships go much poorer than they were wont." Philip's ill-fated Armada of 1588 had given a death-blow to the sea power of Portugal as to that of Spain.

The accession of our James I in 1603 seemed to promise her a respite. Lerma, the all-powerful Spanish minister, saw no reason, with the exception of the English claim to trade in the East Indies, for continuing the war. A large exception, yet within the range of diplomacy. The war-party in England, with Sir Walter Raleigh as their spokesman, fell into discredit; the squadron fitted out against Spanish trade in the last year of Elizabeth was stopped; and King James, in June, 1603, issued a proclamation declaring that all prizes taken from Spain or Portugal after April 24th must be restored. The treaty of peace, signed in 1604, was followed by a further proclamation in 1605 against attacks on Spanish or Portuguese vessels. The pacific spirit reached even to the Indies, and in 1605 the Portuguese captain-general gave the Governor of Manila a warrant to trade with the English.

Then the pendulum swung back. In 1607 Spain informed our ambassador that she could never be friendly with those who traded to the Indies. In 1608 she proposed to occupy the Cape of Good Hope and there to intercept all ships proceeding to the East. In 1609 the truce of Antwerp gave Spain a freer hand with the English, and the wrangle in 1610 - 1611 of the two governments over the Persian ambassador in Europe flamed out in broadsides on the Indian coast.

However King James might hanker after marriages

at Madrid, the English nation had made up its mind that in the Asiatic seas there could be no peace with Portugal. To this conviction Captain Nicholas Downton of the first Joint Stock voyage gave practical effect. Arriving in Suwali Roads off Surat on October 15, 1614, with his four ships, and "not having above four sick men in the whole fleet," he found the Moghul governor

GENERAL VIEW OF DIU.

besieging the Portuguese coast settlements of Daman and Diu. When the governor pressed him to take part against the Portuguese, he refused "for that there was peace between our king and the King of Spain." The Moghul governor replied that if the English would do nothing for him, he would do nothing for them; but Downton sternly declared that he would not be hired to fight the Portuguese, yet would not be withheld from fighting if they attacked him first. The governor accordingly forbade all trade on shore with the English ships.

On December 6, 1614, Downton heard that the Portuguese viceroy at Goa was equipping a great force against him. It was to be on a scale sufficient to crush, without hope of escape, the insolent intruders into the Asiatic seas. Best's fight had taught the Portuguese the unwisdom of engaging the English with anything like equal forces, and the viceroy gathered the naval strength of Portugal in Indian waters for one overwhelming attack. While collecting his armada at Goa he sent on some light vessels to occupy our attention, and on December 23, 1614, twenty-two Portuguese "frigates," or rowed galleys, anchored during the night in the shallows between our ships and the river mouth. They were protected from us by sand-banks, and as traffic with the shore was forbidden by the native governor, Downton could not victual or refit to enable him to take to sea. Moreover, like Best in 1612, he realized the advantage which the more skilful handling of the English ships gave amid the mud-banks and currents of the Tapti estuary. The Portuguese thought they had shut him in among the shoals, and he made the shoals fight for him. By January 18, 1615, the whole Portuguese fleet had arrived, including six great galleons, three smaller ships, two galleys, and sixty "frigates," or rowed barges, with "twenty soldiers apiece and eighteen oars a side." The Viceroy of Goa, Dom Jeronimo de Azevedo, commanded in person, flying his flag as admiral of the Indian seas.

The English were cruelly overmatched. The largest Portuguese galleon was of 800 tons burden and carried

260 fighting men with 28 pieces of ordnance. Five others were of 700 to 400 tons. The "frigates" alone carried about 1200 soldiers in addition to the rowers. The total strength of the armada amounted to 2600 Europeans, whose duty it was to work 234 guns, besides the native crews to the number of 6000, who sailed the ships.

Downton, with his four vessels, 400 men, and 80 guns of much inferior calibre, seemed caught in a trap, with the Moghul governor unfriendly on shore, the "frigates" guarding the shallow entrance to the river, and the great galleons and galleys cutting off retreat to sea. But Downton felt that on that fight depended "all hope of future times;" for if he were defeated, the Portuguese would make peace with the native governor and the English would be expelled from the country for ever.

What troubled him most was the unequal drudgery thrown on his men. The work of the Portuguese ships was done by slaves and "inferior sea-people," while their soldiers remained fresh for battle. The English crews, on the other hand, before actual fighting could begin, "are first tired or half-spent with the labour of the ship, as heaving at capstern, and getting up our anchors . . . making them in hot countries both weary and faint." Downton poured out his heart in secret prayer, "ever as I could be solitary, or free from others, very earnestly craving aid and assistance from the Lord of Hosts." But he showed a bold face to his crews, and asked all the captains and some of the mates of his little squadron to supper—January 19, 1615.

They assembled in a mood not less resolute than his own. Downton's plan was first to weaken the enemy by luring some of them aground, as had happened during Best's fight at the same spot in 1612. Trusting to his superior seamanship, and to the quicker handling of his vessels, he accordingly, on January 20, 1615, sent the *Hope* ahead of his three other ships toward the southern sand, in the expectation that the great galleons would follow to seize her. But the Portuguese admiral, while keeping between her and the sea, avoided the shoals, and Downton, thinking there would be no fighting that day, cast anchor, leaving the *Hope* some way in advance.

The Portuguese swallowed the bait, and beset her with three vessels of light draught and thirty-six "frigates." Before Downton could get clear of his anchors and come up, the enemy had rowed boldly round the *Hope*, fastened themselves to her sides, boarded her thrice, and were thrice beaten back, finding "no quiet here." After the third bloody repulse, unable to unloose their swarm of grappled vessels under the English shot, they set fire to them and leapt overboard, expecting that the *Hope* would perish in the circle of flames. They themselves trusted to be picked up by the galleons, but the fire from the other three English ships which had cut their cables and come to the rescue of the *Hope* prevented succour to the despairing swimmers.

The galleons, now separated at ebb-tide from our ships by a spit of sand, could only fire across it, doing some damage to rigging, but none to the hulls. Meanwhile the flames from the burning vessels caught the mainmast of the *Hope*. By heroic efforts she at length cast them off, and they drifted on to the shoals, burning

AN EARLY ENGLISH WAR-SHIP.
After a painting by Holbein.

to the water's edge. One hard day's battle, January 20, 1615, taught the Portuguese that, if they were to capture our squadron, it must be by fair fighting with their larger ships, and that their mosquito swarm of "frigates" had better keep out of range. They cost us but five men killed; while a Persian reported that the Portuguese sent 350 men ashore to be buried at Daman, and Downton reckoned their loss at one hundred men slain besides those drowned. Next day, the 22d, the Portuguese endeavoured to patch up a truce with the native Governor of Surat, but he, seeing the change of fortune, turned a deaf ear.

The Portuguese then tried a blockade. Their rowed "frigates" held the shallows and partially cut off supplies from the shore, while their great galleons and galleys, with a fighting force many times the number of our whole crews, anchored outside the English. There our four vessels lay, one of them disabled, between the crowd of "frigates" protected by shoals and the line of war-ships to seaward. Downton says it was only the impossibility of renewing the burned mainmast of the *Hope* that prevented his trying his fortune against the Portuguese viceroy in deep water. But each morning and evening he fired off a volley at the enemy, aiming his best cannon at the viceroy's prow—"which I did to try his temper." The capture of the English ships seemed, however, only a question of time. After two weeks of constant watch and patient endurance, on February 3, 1615, writes Downton, "it pleased God, this day, at night when I had least leisure to mourn, to call to his mercy my only son." "The volleys aforesaid appointed to try the temper of the viceroy," he sternly adds, "served also to honour his burial."

But the spectacle of a great armada not daring day after day to attack four small ships had its effect on the native governor's mind, and the Portuguese viceroy found that the English temper could better sustain a blockade than his own could prolong it. So on February 8th, the great galleons, having received further reinforcements, at last came "driving up with the flood" against us, only to "make away as fast as they might" from our guns. The next day, February 9th, after a like attack and retreat (probably a feint), they sent two fire-ships down on our little squadron, in the night. But the frigates that towed them lost heavily under our guns, and hastily cast off the fire-ships, which passed us without harm. On February 10th another attempt with fire-ships and frigates failed. Meanwhile Downton, fearing that the galleons might land their troops and march on Surat, had so disposed his ships as to attack them if they tried to disembark their fighting men.

The Portuguese viceroy reluctantly realized that he was outwitted in strategy and beaten in fighting. On February 11, 1615, his unwieldy galleons, which had been reduced to inaction through fear of the shallows, dropped down southwards to the bar, and on February 13, 1615, the armada sailed away and was no more seen. Downton admits that throughout the long struggle he never saw men fight more bravely than the Portuguese. He himself had obtained supplies from shore by means of country boats, armed by the English factory at Surat—craft which eventually mounted two to six small pieces of cannon and, under the name of grabs or gallivats, became the nucleus of our Indian navy.

The Moghul governor watched the progress of the fighting, and probably felt that Downton's strategy had saved Surat from a land-attack by the Portuguese. He now threw himself heartily on the side of the English, pitched his camp with great state on the shore close to our ships, and amid mutual congratulations and Homeric pledges exchanged his Eastern sword "with hilt of massie gold," wrote Downton, for his own less costly English side-arms. After friendly entreaties to delay his departure, Captain Downton sailed for Bantam and there died on August 6, 1615; leaving a name never surpassed for endurance and skilful valour. He had established the supremacy of the English over the Portuguese on the Indian coast. Next year, 1616, Captain Keeling boldly entered into a treaty with the Zamorin of Calicut to seize the neighbouring Portuguese settlements and to hand one of them over to the English.

PORTUGUESE RESIDENTS AT BANTAM.

It is not needful to follow step by step the decline of a gallant enemy. If the Portuguese, unwillingly linked to the decaying Spanish monarchy, could no longer conquer, they knew how to die. In 1616 a great carrack, carrying an admiral's flag, fought four smaller English vessels for three days; replying to our summons to surrender that "Don Meneses had promised his master, the King of Spain, not to quit his ship: out of which he might be forced, but never commanded."

During two nights he hung out a lantern to show his track to his enemies; on the third the battered hull drove upon the rocks and was set fire to by the remnants of her crew.

But valour could not stay the cancer of misrule. The abuse of patronage which had shipped off young women from Lisbon with the gift of an Indian appointment as their dowry for a husband to be picked up at Goa, reached its height after the forced union of Portugal with Spain in 1580. The sale of Indian offices was an illicit trade at the Court of Philip II; under Philip III of Spain it became a source of the public revenue. The Lisbon fleet of 1614 carried orders to the Goa viceroy "that all commands and high appointments that would be likely to yield money were to be put up to sale, there being then no other visible means whereby to provide for the wants of the administration." Old incumbents were ruthlessly dispossessed, and were succeeded by men who clutched at everything to repay the price of their unstable appointments. In 1637, and perhaps on other occasions, the auction included the command of fortresses. In 1618 two English ships took a Portuguese carrack with £517,500 in specie, "which was the pay of all the soldiers in the East Indies," according to the records in the State Papers. The Spanish kings began to look upon the East Indies as a mere drain to their silver supply from America, and the stories of their indifference to Portuguese interests in Asia border on the incredible. During the three years that Fernão de Albuquerque was viceroy at Goa,

1619-1622, he is said to have received not a single letter of instruction or information from the court of Spain.

Yet in this very viceroyalty a catastrophe had taken place which might have stung even Spain into a spasm of remorseful energy. Ormuz, the pearl of Portuguese Asia, fell to the English. During the century since Albuquerque captured the island in 1515, the Portuguese had dealt with it as their own, and dominated from its fortress the entrance to the Persian Gulf. Of the treaties by which they bound the princes of Ormuz I have already spoken. On the death of a king of Ormuz, says a Venetian traveller, Cesare de' Federici, *circ.* 1565, "the captain of the Portugals chooseth another of the blood-royal," and "sweareth him to be true" "to the King of Portugal as his Lord and Governor." Their oppressions and piracies had led the Shah of Persia to appeal for help to France in 1603, and seven years later to England. In 1618 a trade was opened between our agents at Surat and the port of Jask, near the entrance to the Persian Gulf, and in 1620 James I addressed a letter to Shah Abbas with a view to obtaining a factory on shore. The Portuguese opposed our ships as usual with a greatly superior force, and in November, 1620, the English gained a victory which made them a recognized power in the Persian Gulf.

The Persian governor determined to use us against the general oppressor—the Portuguese—and in 1621 refused to allow our ships to embark their cargoes until we agreed to join with him in an attack on Ormuz. The blow was delivered early in the following year. Five ships and four pinnaces of the English Company defeated the Portuguese fleet in the Persian Gulf, and in concert with a Persian land-force captured Ormuz. On April 27, 1622, the 2500 survivors of the Portuguese garrison were shipped off to Goa in vessels compassion-

GOMBROON, OR BUNDER ABBAS, ON THE PERSIAN GULF.

ately given by the English, who with difficulty protected them from the vengeance of the natives. In spite of our efforts, the unfortunate men were stripped and maltreated by the Persians. Shah Abbas rewarded the English by a settlement on the mainland of Persia at Gombroon, afterwards called Bunder Abbas in his honour, and gave them a patent for half the customs duties, the first of those revenue grants which were to end in the transfer of great Indian provinces to British administration.

Thus went down the power of Portugal in 1622 in

the Persian Gulf, as it had gone down before the English in 1612 and 1615 on the Indian coast. In the last years of her proud nationality, Portugal had divided her Asiatic empire into three governments (1571): the coast of East Africa, India with the Persian Gulf from Cape Guardafui to Ceylon, and the Eastern Archipelago with its headquarters at Malacca. Nine years later (1580) she was forced into union with Spain, and within a generation a new power from the North had broken her chain of Asiatic possessions at the middle link. Her two other governments on the African coast and in the Eastern Archipelago, thus thrust asunder, became an easy prey. From 1622, India and the Persian Gulf lay open to England so far as Portugal was concerned. Before Portugal could break loose from Spain and reassert her independence in 1640, her supremacy in the Asiatic seas had become a legend of the past. In 1642 she partially, and in 1654 she finally, accepted the situation, and agreed that the English should have the right to reside and trade in all her Eastern possessions. The treaty which assured this latter agreement was one entered into between Oliver Cromwell and King John IV of Portugal, and dated at Westminster, July 10, 1654. It has a special importance as marking the end of the old Portuguese monopoly and formulating the new policy of England in the East.

AN ALMADIA.

CHAPTER III

THE STRUGGLE BETWEEN THE ENGLISH AND THE DUTCH FOR THE EASTERN ARCHIPELAGO

1601 - 1623

OUR real struggle for the Indian trade was to be with a very different rival. The decline of Spain and Portugal left the two Protestant sea-powers of the North face to face in the Asiatic seas. Holland entered on the contest in the patriotic flush of achieved independence, and with the same newly born sense of national unity which nerved Portugal for her heroic explorations two hundred years before. England had left behind her the spacious age of Elizabeth; before her stretched the crooked diplomacy and domestic disorders of a dynasty which could never become English at heart, and which had in the end to be cast forth. Throughout the first half of the seventeenth century the States-General played the leading maritime part in Europe, as the Portuguese House of Aviz had played it in the first half of the sixteenth.

The magnificent position which Holland thus won,

she merited by her services to mankind. It is scarcely too much to say that the political reformation of Europe dates from the Dutch Declaration of Independence in 1581. Then for the first time was asserted and enforced the principle that governments exist for nations, not nations for governments, as no abstract dogma, but as a truth for which a whole people was willing to die.

The vigour which achieved the liberty of Holland pulsed through every vein of her internal and external life. Amsterdam, the city of refuge from Parma's havoc at Antwerp, became the European emporium of Indian commerce, richer and more powerful by far than Venice, Genoa, or Lisbon in their prime. Her manufactures were improved and her financial strength increased by the Jews who fled the Spanish Inquisition, and who gave to Amsterdam alike the genius of Spinoza and the diamond-cutting industry which centres there to this day. Dutch navigators put a girdle of discovery and colonization round the globe from New Holland, now Australia, to New Amsterdam, now New York. Dutch agriculture, by transferring the potato and turnip from the garden to the field, created a new winter food for men and cattle, as has been pointed out by the political economist Thorold Rogers. This change made possible the growth of population in modern Europe, feeding threefold the inhabitants off areas which had barely supported one-third in frequent peril of famine, and contributing more than any other cause to banish leprosy from Christendom. At the same time the Dutch leaped forward to the front rank of intellectual activity. Holland became the printing house of Europe. Her thinkers were the oracles of their age, her painters have left an imperishable influence on art. Leyden was more famous for a time than Oxford or Paris, and it is still a tradition of the Scottish Bar to complete a legal education at the great Dutch university.

The outburst of national energy found its chief vent on the sea. The Indian voyage of De Houtman in 1595 fired the popular enthusiasm, and while the London merchants were awaiting the changing moods of Elizabeth, or extracting subscriptions for a single expedition, no fewer than fifteen fleets sailed between 1595 and 1601 from Holland to the East. This period of "separate" Dutch voyages is so little realized by English historians, yet forms so essential a part of the Dutch precedent closely followed by the English Company, that I give their details below.[1] Of the sixty-five ships sent from Holland in the six years from April, 1595, to May, 1601, Amsterdam supplied by far the larger number; Zeeland, with Middleburg as its centre, came next; and the merchants of minor states competed with companies of their own.

The Dutch government sagaciously foresaw the dangers to which separate expeditions might give rise in distant and hostile seas: that opposition of interests among rival groups of adventurers of the same nation, and that weakness in the face of a common enemy, to which the English system of "separate voyages" subsequently succumbed. On March 20, 1602, as we have

[1] For this information see Appendix II, A.

seen, it united the Indian Companies in the several states into one Joint Stock Association under the title of the United East India Company, with an exclusive monopoly of the Indian trade for twenty-one years, dating from January 1, 1602.

The combination was compulsory, as any company which refused to join would be *ipso facto* shut out from the Indian trade. On the other hand, the Dutch government behaved liberally to the separate organizations, and took over their directors for life into the joint directorate of the United Company. In this way the number of directors of the United Company, although fixed in permanence under the charter at sixty, was at first seventy-three. All this will become clear to any one who will take the pains to consult the Dutch records on the subject.

In a similar spirit the joint directorate was divided into six chambers, representing the six subscribing states in proportion to the amount which they severally contributed to the common capital. This representative principle was carried still further in the executive Committee of Seventeen entrusted with the management of the United Company's expeditions. Sixteen of its members were taken from the six subscribing provincial centres in direct ratio to their contributions, while the seventeenth was appointed by the minor states in succession.

The government had close relations with the personnel of the directorate. Reports were made to the States-General; accounts were to be submitted to them;

they supervised the Company's instructions to its servants; and they left in the hands of the Company until 1638 a sum of twenty-five thousand florins (£2000) due for the charter of 1602. The Council of Seventeen was, in fact, a sort of elected Board of Control, intermediate between the Dutch Company and the States-General, somewhat, although by no means exactly, like the Board of Control established nearly two centuries later between the English East India Company and Parliament.

The qualification for a director in the four leading Chambers was £500 and £250 in the two minor ones. The directors and their staff were to be remunerated by one per cent. on the cargoes. A general reckoning was to be made every ten years, at which periods shareholders might reclaim their subscriptions and withdraw. The shares were ordinary ones of £250 each, and "head-participant" shares of £500. The subscription was thrown open to the whole population of Holland. But practically the first expedition in 1602 consisted of the ships belonging to the previous separate companies and taken over from them by the United Dutch Company.

So high rose the tide of national enthusiasm that even ruined Antwerp, bleeding and mangled in the claws of Spain, found money for shares. Her clandestine subscriptions, through agents at Amsterdam and Middelburg, roused the wrath of her oppressors, and an Antwerp merchant was condemned to lifelong imprisonment for this offence. The great Company, with its capital of, say, £540,000, and with ample powers of conquest or attack vested in it by the State, was recognized by friend and foe as a new national force. It marks, in truth, the final development of that policy of sea-war by sea-trade with which Holland had first confronted, and was now about to beat down, Spain.

The States-General perfectly understood that there could be no peace between the two nations. It was not merely a question of the sullen Spanish pride, and of the long slaughter of Protestant saints and patriots in sacked towns and on bloody fields; it was also the spectral procession of those one hundred thousand judicial murders of peaceful men and women by fire and torture and burying alive, before the country rose in its despair, that compelled every act of Holland to be an act of war against Spain. The United East India Company was the instrument by which the Dutch were to compel the oppressor first to an unwilling truce, and finally to let them go.

That magnificent achievement belongs to European history, and I here venture only to note a few of the first landmarks which it left behind in Asia. In 1602 the fleet of the Dutch Company routed the Portuguese near Bantam, and laid open for ever the road to the Moluccas or Spice Islands. From that date the ascendency of the Dutch in the Eastern seas, although subject to occasional checks, was only a question of time.

In 1603 they threatened Goa, the middle capital of the Indo-Portuguese route, and in 1606 blockaded its western terminus by carrying the war into the estuary of the Tagus itself. They shut up that river by a great expedition, to which the Dutch East India Company largely contributed, and in April, 1607, they totally destroyed the Spanish fleet in Gibraltar Bay. In the furthermost East, the Dutch wrenched the fairest isles of the Moluccas from the Portuguese, and although partially expelled for a time, they returned in force,

A BIRD'S-EYE VIEW OF BANTAM.

gradually completed the conquest, and ousted the Portuguese trade even in Japan.

The exclusive possession of the Spice Islands became a fixed point in the Dutch policy. The instructions to their first governor-general, Pieter Both (1609-1614), were that "the commerce of the Moluccas, Amboyna, and Banda should belong to the Company, and that no other nation in the world should have the least part." Throughout their long negotiations with England, they never yielded their sovereign rights in the Spice Islands.

Having thus struck at Spain at the two extremities

of her Indo-Portuguese trade, Lisbon and the Moluccas, the Dutch proceeded deliberately to establish themselves at vantage-posts along the line of communication. Into the military operations of the next half-century space precludes me from entering. Five dates must suffice to mark the further Dutch conquest of the Indian trade-route. Having made themselves a power in Java, midway between the Malay Straits and the Moluccas, they fixed their capital at Batavia on its northern coast, in 1619. In 1641 they captured Malacca from the Portuguese, and thus turned the straits into a Dutch waterway. From 1638 onwards they expelled the Portuguese from Ceylon, driving them from their last stronghold in 1658. They took possession of the great half-way house of Indo-European commerce, the Cape of Good Hope, and settled a colony there in 1652. When Portugal emerged, in 1640, from her sixty years' captivity to Spain, she found that her power in the Eastern seas had passed to the Dutch. In 1641 she surrendered for ever her exclusive claims to the spice trade by a treaty with Holland, on the basis of the Dutch retaining their conquests, and of free navigation and trade to both powers in the Eastern seas.

Holland's conquest of the Indian Archipelago was, in truth, a conquest by treaty not less than by war. Always ready to fight, she regarded fighting chiefly as an instrument of trade. Her object was not, as Portugal's had been, to take vengeance on the "*nefandissimi Machometi secta*" for the loss of the Holy Places in Palestine, or to swell the pride of a royal house by new Asiatic titles and to bring the kingdoms of the East within the Christian fold, but by establishing a sufficient degree of sovereignty over the islands to prevent them from selling their spices to any European nation but herself. Where she found a stringent supremacy needful, she established it; where a less control sufficed, she was at first willing to leave the princes and peoples very much to themselves. The whole process is laid bare in the documents copied for the English East India Company during our occupation of Java (1811 - 1818) and now preserved in the India Office.

I intend, as in my sketch of the Portuguese policy in Asia, to exhibit briefly from the manuscript records the methods, rather than the military operations, by which the Dutch built up their supremacy in the Eastern seas. So far as it is possible to generalize, the Dutch kept three points steadily in view. First, the sovereign authority of Holland must be acknowledged by the island-chiefs. This was asserted sometimes as the result of conquest, but frequently in the form of a protectorate, the native princes consenting to hold their territories as a kind of fief under the Dutch suzerainty. Second, all other European nations, and especially England, were to be excluded from the island trade; and in many cases specific engagements were entered into for war against Portugal and Spain. Third, as the Dutch tightened their grasp on the Archipelago, they adopted more drastic provisions for the maintenance of their monopoly. The natives were forbidden to sail beyond certain limits from their respective coasts, under pain of piracy; they were prohib-

THE OLD EAST INDIA HOUSE USED AS THE SIGN OF A "JOINER."

ited from trading with Indian or other Asiatic ports; and they were compelled to root up their spice-trees in islands which competed with the produce of the Dutch settlements. Stipulations were sometimes introduced to permit the introduction of the Reformed Religion.

A few examples must suffice to illustrate these general principles of policy. The arena was that great island world, perhaps the mountain-tops and plateaus of a submerged continent, which stretches from the shores of Asia to the Australian coast. An almost continuous belt of long islands (Sumatra, Java, Flores and Timor, and others) curves southeastwards from the Malay Peninsula to the northwest point of Australia. Within this belt, on the north, lie Borneo; Celebes to the east of Borneo; the Moluccas or Spice Islands, including Ternate and Tidore; with the valuable Nutmeg and Clove Isles, Banda, Amboyna, Pulaway, Pularoon, and Rosengyn among them to the south; and finally New Guinea at the easternmost extremity. The Philippines stretch in elongated broken masses northward from the Spice Islands toward Formosa, China, and Japan.

The Dutch resolved to make themselves masters both of the outer or southern belt of long islands and of the rich spice archipelago which they girt in. A glance at the map will show that the first strategic point on the outer belt is Achin, on the northwestern point of Sumatra, commanding the entrance to the narrow sea between that island and the Malay Peninsula. The King of Achin claimed a disputed supremacy over all Sumatra, and in 1600 the Dutch entered into a treaty with him for a resident factory. The relations were gradually strengthened into an armed alliance against the Portuguese, whose Eastern capital, Malacca, dominated the opposite coast. When the Dutch grew strong and the Achin raja, fearing the results of their success, began to give trouble, he found his dependent chiefdoms and islets had themselves entered into separate engagements with Holland acknowledging her sovereignty, and securing to her the privileges of exclusive trade. From the year 1688 onward, and even before that date, the Dutch treaties with the Sumatra minor chiefs pledged them to hostility against the King of Achin.

On the opposite coast of the Malay Peninsula the Dutch took even more effective measures. The keys to the passage on the northern side were Portuguese Malacca, about two-thirds down the straits, and the native kingdom of Johor, at their exit near the eastern point of the Malay Peninsula. In the early days of the Dutch Company, Malacca, the Eastern capital of Portuguese Asia, could defy any Protestant fleet unless aided by a native land power. So in 1606 the Dutch made a compact with Johor to seize Malacca; Holland to keep the town and fortress, Johor to have the adjacent territory, and all captured property to be divided between them. From this time onward the Dutch could attack Malacca with the help of the Achin fleet from Sumatra on the northwest and of the Johor levies from the east. It was only their unstable relations with these native states that deferred the final fall of the Portuguese headquarters in the Far East to Holland in 1641. In that year the country around Malacca also abjured its allegiance to Portugal and promised fidelity to the Dutch.

Of scarcely less importance than the Malacca passage between the Malay Peninsula and Sumatra, which thus came into Dutch keeping, were the Straits of Sunda between Sumatra and Java. This narrow opening formed an alternative entrance through the belt of long islands into the Archipelago, and the Dutch Company resolved to secure the command of it. Bantam, on the northwestern point of Java, dominated its exit into the inner sea of islands. Even before the United Company's first voyage, the "separate" Dutch commanders had made a compact with the Raja of Bantam for "mutual honest trade," and the subsequent treaties with Bantam fill many pages of the India Office records.

In 1609, by an engagement known as the "Eternal Treaty," the Dutch agreed to aid the Bantam raja against foreign enemies, particularly the Spanish and Portuguese, and his state slowly passed into a dependency of Holland. The Dutch perceived, however, that the mouth of the Jacatra River, with its spacious bay, a little to the east of Bantam, afforded superior convenience for shipping. In 1612 a treaty secured free trade to the Dutch at Jacatra, and after a scuffle with the English, the Dutch destroyed the old Javanese town, rebuilt it under the name of Batavia, and made it their headquarters in the East (1619).

The clearness of vision which led them to secure the two main inlets into the Archipelago (the Straits of Malacca and the Straits of Sunda) also guided the

Dutch to the best sites in the enclosed island world. The positions which they took up were either strong for war or rich in trade, and eventually passed into the

A CHINESE STREET IN BATAVIA, JAVA.
(Copyright by Underwood and Underwood, New York.)

Dutch power by conquest from the Portuguese or by treaties with the native chiefs. Almost everywhere we find a defensive alliance with the natives against the Portuguese becomes the basis of the Dutch power. Thus at Ternate, the chief seat of trade in the Moluccas or Spice Islands, the Sultan entered into a treaty with the Dutch admiral in 1607 for protection against a Spanish-Portuguese armada. The right to build and to destroy forts followed. The uprooting of the clove-trees which might compete with the Dutch at Amboyna came in due course; and in 1649 the Sultan appointed the Dutch governor as his viceroy over his chief island dependencies.

One other example must suffice. Amboyna, the richest clove island of the Southern Moluccas, had been visited by the Dutch "separate" expeditions, and entered into a trade arrangement. In 1600 this friendly relation was strengthened into a compact for the expulsion of the Portuguese and the erection of a Dutch castle. In 1605 the chiefs acknowledged the sovereignty of Holland, in return for a guarantee of protection against Portugal and Spain. They agreed to aid the Dutch in their wars and to sell their cloves to no other nation. As the Dutch drew tighter their bonds on the Moluccas, Amboyna, like its suzerain island, Ternate, grew restive. But in 1618 the Dutch finally established their supremacy at Amboyna, and secured by treaties the exclusive trade, the free exercise of the Reformed Religion, and the right to demand forced labour. In 1628 they took advantage of a dispute in the family of the Ternate raja to shake off his suzerain claims to the customs duties at Amboyna, and to declare themselves masters of the island by virtue of conquest from the Portuguese in 1605.

The harsher measures of the Dutch in the Archipelago belong, generally, to a period subsequent to 1623. It was not till a much later date that they fully developed their system of confining the islanders on pain of piracy to their own or adjacent coasts, forbade their sending or receiving embassies to or from India and the Asiatic continent, and enforced a tribute in "full-grown slaves." In the early years of the seventeenth century the Dutch really were what they declared themselves to be, the deliverers of the islands from Portuguese oppression. In return for their protection they demanded the exclusive trade and such subsidiary guarantees as they deemed needful to secure it.

The growing rivalry of the English put an end to this state of comparative calm. On the one hand, the Dutch claimed the monopoly of the richest of the Spice Islands on the threefold ground of priority of occupation, services rendered to the natives against the Portuguese, and treaties which at once defined and secured their rights. On the other hand, the English asserted the still earlier arrival of Drake's ship in 1579, denied that the isolated coast castles of the Dutch amounted to effective occupation of a great archipelago, and claimed an equal right with the Dutch to make treaties with the native powers.

The English claim founded on Drake's priority of discovery could not be pressed in serious diplomacy, as it told against our general contention that a title to territory could be maintained only on the ground of actual possession, or effective occupation. But it long served as a national rallying cry. In 1606 Sir Henry Middleton asserted our right to a factory in the Moluccas, " for that Sir Francis Drake had trade in Ternate

SIR FRANCIS DRAKE.

before the name of the Hollanders was known in those parts of the world." As late as 1652 it formed a basis of a discourse, the *East India Trade first discovered by the English*, in which the author gravely relates how the Dutch " took the advantage of the negligent and inconsiderate English " to secure the profits of Drake's discovery. This popular plea, although put forward in official documents, cannot be accepted by an honest historian. But it explains that sense of having been overreached which embittered English feeling to the Dutch.

The situation was in fact incompatible with peace. Yet Holland and England were not only at peace in Europe, but were the joint champions of a great religious cause. Nor could either country at once forget that, but for Elizabeth's coldness to the Dutch overtures, the English queen might have been the sovereign of the united nations. On the arrival of the English ships in the East in 1602, the commanders of the two Protestant fleets joined against the Portuguese; and, as we saw, the plunder of a Portugal ship supplied the return cargo for the first voyage of the London Company. But the Dutch quickly perceived that the English were both weak and inconvenient neighbours in the Archipelago. Each English voyage worked with a small capital, and raised the local prices by eagerness to secure a freight. The Dutch abstained for a time from hostilities, yet strove to frighten the natives from dealing with the newcomers by representing them as buccaneers. When the island chiefs found that the English, instead of making piratical descents, came with money in their hands, and parted with it more freely than the Dutch, this device failed. The Dutch next tried bribery, and in 1603 were said to have offered twelve thousand dollars to the natives of Pularoon if they would not trade with the English. The death of Elizabeth in 1603, and

King James's treaty with Spain and Portugal in the following year, broke the tradition of Dutch and English friendship based on the joint championship of the Protestant cause. Scruples of sentiment or of religion disappeared, and commercial rivalry became the permanent factor in the relations of England and Holland.

It is not needful to dwell on the early phases of the struggle which ensued. The English Company was the weakling child of the old age of Elizabeth and of the shifty policy of King James; the Dutch Company was the strong outgrowth of the life and death struggle of a new nation with its Spanish oppressors. The English Company began with slender resources in 1601 the system of "separate voyages," which the Dutch Company, after a trial of that method on a great scale after 1595, deliberately abandoned in 1602 for the joint system of a United Company with vast capital—the joint system which the English adopted only after eleven years of painful experience in 1612, and even then in a less stable form.

Yet the English boldly stood forth to the natives not only as rivals but as opponents of the Dutch. In 1605 the King of Tidore, in the Spice Islands, appealed to King James for help against the Hollanders, on the ground that his Majesty was in friendship with Spain. The King of Ternate, hard by, inquired after the health of the "great Captain Francis Drake," whose return "we have daily expected," and complained that the Dutch, having driven out the Portuguese, prevented him from granting a factory to the English. The King of Bantam in Java rejoiced that "now England and Bantam are both as one." From Achin in Sumatra, commanding the western gateway of the Archipelago, to the Spice Islands in its farthest east, the Dutch found themselves encountered by a new set of competing, and sometimes hostile, compacts between the native princes and the English Company.

We even went so far as to try to provide an English wife for the King of Sumatra. As that potentate had expressed a wish for such a consort, "a gentleman of honourable parentage" proposed at a court meeting of the Company in 1614, "his daughter of most excellent parts for music, her needle, and good discourse, as also very beautiful and personable." The probable benefit to the Company was gravely debated, "and the lawfulness of the enterprise proved by Scripture." But, as the State Papers show, some feared that the other wives "may poison her if she became an extraordinary favourite." The father was willing to take the risk, but we do not hear that the lady went out. Yet the bare suggestion must have seemed alarming to the Dutch.

Nor did the English diplomacy in Europe tend to soothe the rivalry in the Asiatic seas. Holland quickly valued at its real worth the lip-friendship of King James. During the Dutch efforts for a settlement with Spain, England was detached from the Protestant cause by the bait of a Spanish marriage, and of the Netherlands as a prospective dowry of the Infanta after the death of the childless archduke. Holland, thus deserted, saw her hoped-for peace with Spain dwindle to the Twelve Years' Truce of 1609, leaving the menace of a Spanish war on its expiration, and a resentment against England for a century to come.

The Dutch in the East took prompt measures to deal with the situation. If England proved so faint a friend in Europe, the Archipelago was to become a place of little ease for the English Company. Scarcely had the Spanish truce of 1609 given Holland a breathing-pause than she resolved to consolidate her Asiatic settlements

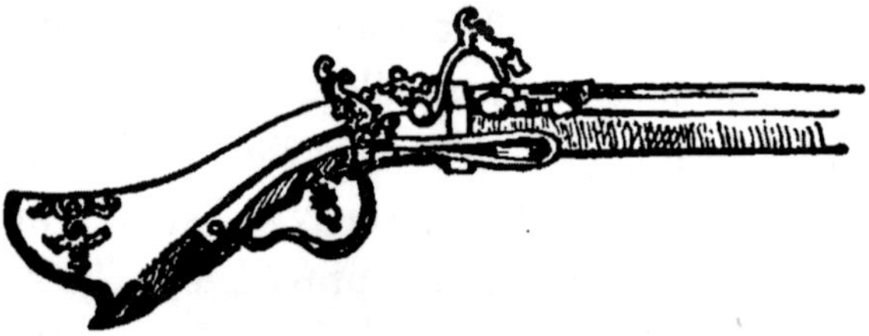

A GUN FROM THE INDIAN ARCHIPELAGO.

under a firm local control. The Council of Seventeen nominated Pieter Both, a man of great ability, to the charge of the Company's factories, and in November, 1609, the States-General commissioned him with extensive powers as the first governor-general of the Dutch East Indies. Pieter Both justified their confidence. He had proved his capacity as admiral of the Brabant Company's expedition in 1599-1601, and his initial duty in his new high office was to take an oath of fidelity of the Dutch servants in the East to the States-General and the United Company.

He sailed as governor-general with a fleet of eight ships in January, 1610, and after months of storm arrived at Bantam in January, 1611. During the next four years he brought the islands within a network of treaties. He thus confirmed from Java to the Moluccas the supremacy and exclusive trade of the Dutch; procured, when expedient, the toleration of the Protestant religion; and laid the foundations of a new national power in the Eastern Archipelago. On the expiration of his office, he sailed in January, 1615, with four richly laden vessels for Europe, but perished in a hurricane off the Mauritius. The name of a mountain in that island long commemorated his loss, and appears in a journal of 1689 as "Pierre Both."

He had found his task an easy one. The native rulers in the Archipelago, like the coast rajas with whom the Portuguese dealt on the Malabar seaboard, were princes on a small scale. The greatest of them, like the King of Achin and the Sultan of Ternate, exercised an uncertain suzerainty over detached territories and islands, each with lesser chiefs of its own. Nor as regards the English did the first Dutch governor-general find much difficulty. The whole number of English ships sent out up to the year 1610, inclusive, amounted to seventeen, and of the seventeen vessels only a few were at any one time in Asiatic waters. The Dutch, on the other hand, had sent out sixty-five ships before the union of the separate companies in 1602, and sixty-nine vessels from 1602 to 1610. The armament and fighting force of the English ships were also inferior to the Dutch. The Dutch, moreover, took a practical care for the well-being and morals of their servants that was unknown in the English factories. While the London Company sent out volumes of sermons and forced back the first English wife, the Dutch governor-general carried with him thirty-six goodly young women as mates to their countrymen in the East. It was not till more than half a century later that the English Company, moved by the scandal of a half-caste population, followed their example.

The English factors and captains in the Archipelago were in truth outmatched at every point, and the London Company found itself compelled to seek support nearer home. In 1611 it opened negotiations at Amsterdam. A letter of Robert Middleton to the burgomasters of that city proposed "that as our nations have long continued in firm bonds and league of amity, so we might peaceably proceed to trade jointly together without troubling of either states." The Dutch replied in an amicable spirit, and proposed to approach the States-General on the subject. But meanwhile the London merchants realized that the struggle was a national one, not to be settled by the two Companies alone, and had declared to the Lord High Treasurer of England that they "are enforced at last to break silence and complain their griefs."

The tale they told was one to which no English sovereign could turn a deaf ear. They had "long and patiently endured sundry notorious wrongs and injurious courses at the hands of the Hollanders," and being now reduced to extremities "but having no means of remedy, do humbly implore your Lordship's honourable assistance and mediation to the States." They based their claim to trade in the Archipelago on the prior discoveries of Drake, Cavendish, and Lancaster; and on Drake's compact with the King of Ternate (the suzerain of the Moluccas) long before the Dutch were heard of in those seas. The argument had its inconveniences, for it would have told still more strongly in favour of the Portuguese prior rights which the English Company were about to scatter to the winds. But it sufficed to bring the question within the range of European diplomacy, and to open out new opportunities to James in his favourite rôle of the peacemaking monarch.

THOMAS CAVENDISH.

From this period the relations of the Dutch and English Companies divide into two distinct branches: continuous negotiation in Europe, and continuous contests in the East. After preliminary action by our ambassador in Holland, the States-General, in 1613, sent commissioners accompanied by Grotius, then pensionary of Rotterdam and the foremost international jurist of the age, to treat with English commissioners in London. Much wrangling resulted in a vague agreement in 1614 that each nation should enjoy such places as it had conquered or discovered, and pay customs duties to the other at those ports, while both should join against the common enemy—Spain and Portugal. The governor of the English Company held a conference with the Dutch ambassador in London for "a loving and friendly trade both defensive and offensive," by the two corporations: we to throw open the Cambay coast to the Dutch, and they to admit us to the Spice Islands.

The growing animosities in the East rendered this arrangement a dead-letter, and in January, 1615, negotiations were renewed at The Hague. Sir Henry Wotton, our ambassador in Holland, together with certain commissioners to represent the East India Company, received a favourable audience from Barneveldt, who would gladly have seen the two Companies join "to beat the Spaniard out of the East Indies." King James himself put pressure on the English Company to come to terms, but forbade any open breach with Spain. This last condition rendered a real agreement impossible for Holland. The English commissioners demanded free trade by the law of nations. The Dutch replied that any trade at all in the Eastern seas could be secured only by great armaments and garrisons against Spain, and that if the English refused to share in the cost, they could not fairly claim to share in the profits.

Finally Barneveldt offered three alternatives. First, for the English to retire from the trade; second, for the English to unite in a joint East India Company with the Dutch; third, for the English to maintain their position by a vigorous war. He declared that the

States-General regarded the East Indian trade as a cardinal point in their national policy, and that they assisted the Dutch Company with great sums to maintain it by force of arms. The English, on the other hand, thought that the Dutch capital was wasted in wars and on an army of ten thousand soldiers in the East. Nothing remained but for our commissioners to come away. The negotiations of 1615 broke down at The Hague, as those of 1613-1614 had proved fruitless in London.

King James felt annoyed that he had failed in his part of royal peacemaker, and the Dutch were aware of the fact. They saw their advantage in a union which should compel the English to share in the Protestant defence of the Indies, and they had confidence in their own ability to retain the lion's share of the trade. They therefore transferred the scene of operations once more to England, and their ambassador urged as a "groundwork" for the amalgamation of the two Companies that they should jointly subscribe £1,200,000 to a common stock. The English Company had by this time broken the Spanish-Portuguese power on the Indian coast, and saw their way to trade without sharing in the costly armaments and island-defences of the Dutch. In August, 1615, they declared that they were content that Holland should surcease from her wars with Spain in the East, being themselves "confident that in time they will eat the Spaniard out of that trade, only by underselling him in all parts of Christendom." So with "good words" they thanked the Dutch ambassador, and the third series of negotiations came to an end.

Meanwhile the Hollanders were rendering our position intolerable in the Archipelago. In 1613 they forcibly prevented the people of Machian in the Moluccas from trading with us. In 1614 our agents retaliated by

BROACH, ON THE COAST OF INDIA, IN 1778.

a treaty with the rich nutmeg island Banda, whose inhabitants declared themselves willing to live and die with the English. In 1615 the London Company encouraged its factors to break boldly into the Spice Islands and to attempt both Banda and Amboyna. But the Dutch replied by the argument of "seven tall ships" in the Archipelago, and threatened to sink any English interloper. In December, 1615, at their headquarters at Bantam in Java, "the envy of the Hollanders is so great that to take out one of our eyes they will lose both their own." In 1617 came the news that the Dutch had forty or fifty English prisoners in irons at Amboyna, starving on a single cake of bread a day, so that they were reduced to skin and bone.

The personal hatred between the agents of the two Companies had now risen to fever-heat. The English despised the phlegmatic " mechanic " ways of the Hollanders, called them " shoemakers " and " beer-brewers," and flew into a passion at the mere sight of a Dutch document. In 1618 our admiral at Batavia, Sir Thomas Dale, on receiving a communication in Flemish, " scolded, stamped on the ground, swore, cursed," asking " why the letters were not in French, Spanish, Latin, or any other language if we did not like to write English." The Dutch paid back abuse with scorn, pulled down the English flag, befouled it, and tore it to pieces, and hit upon a device for rendering it hateful to the natives. In 1617 they " covered all the seas from the Red Sea to the coast of China, spoiling and robbing all nations in the name and under the colour of the English." In 1618 they publicly insulted our flag by running up the French and English colours, with Prince Maurice's banner displayed above, " triumphing in the doing thereof, because they have overcome both."

If we look only to their position in the East, they had cause for exultation. Their second governor-general, Gerard Reynst (1614 - 1615), proved a worthy successor to Pieter Both. A director of the United Company at Amsterdam, Reynst was induced to accept the governor-generalship by liberal allowances, a gold medal with a massy chain, and the assurance of being reappointed a director on his return. He sailed in July, 1613, at the head of a large fleet, with ample powers from the Council of Seventeen ratified by the States-General, and with a commission direct from Prince Maurice. This double sanction of the States-General and of the House of Orange represented the union of the supreme civil power with the highest military authority in Holland. It gave to the Flemish Company a national basis which was absent from the charters of our Stuart kings, and which the English Company only obtained by Acts of Parliament under Dutch William, three-quarters of a century later. The tenure of office for the Dutch governor-generals was five years —a term afterwards adopted for our own.

Thus backed by the strength of his nation, Reynst detached a squadron on the voyage out to plant factories at Aden and on the Arabian coast, and became the founder of the Dutch trade in the Red Sea. But his chief aim was to shut up the nutmeg and clove islands of the Archipelago against the English. With a fleet of eleven ships he chastised the Banda chiefs who had traded with us, seized on the neighbouring islands, and drove us out of Amboyna. His career was cut short by dysentery in December, 1615. Laurens Reaal (1616-1618), provisionally appointed to fill his place by the Council of India then assembled at Ternate, consolidated what his two predecessors had won. He strengthened the Dutch fortifications throughout the Archipelago, extended the Company's commerce, filled its exchequer, and prepared the way for the great governor-general who succeeded him.

The English Company also armed itself for a life or death struggle. In spite of obstacles the four expeditions of its First Joint Stock (1613 - 1616) were bring-

ADEN.
(Copyright by Underwood and Underwood, New York.)

ing home rich cargoes, and its shares rose to 207 per cent. in 1617. But much of its property then remained in the Indies, and, owing to losses from the Dutch, had eventually to be sold to the Second Joint Stock at a low valuation. Its accounts could not be finally wound up until 1621, and its whole profits during the eight years (1613 - 1621) only amounted to 87½ per cent. Its permanent achievement, as we shall see, was the strengthening of our position not in the Eastern Archipelago, but on the west coast of India under the sanction of the Moghul emperor obtained by Sir Thomas Roe. In 1616, however, its credit stood high, and the expectations from the division of its profits still higher.

When, therefore, on the expiration of the four years of the First Joint Stock (1613 - 1616), the London Company resolved to open a new contribution for another four years, it was eagerly subscribed. The spirit of adventure among the English nobility and country gentry, which had found scope on the Spanish main under Elizabeth, but which the Spanish entanglements of James pent up, sought an outlet in the Second Joint Stock of the East India Company. Fifteen dukes and earls, thirteen countesses and ladies of title, eighty-two knights, judges and privy councillors, headed the list of 954 subscribers. The contributions amounted to £1,629,040, the largest capital that had ever been subscribed to any joint stock undertaking in the world. With this sum, to be divided into three voyages, it seemed as if the English Company might at length hold their own against Holland in the Eastern seas.

They soon discovered, however, that the capture of the spice trade was not to be achieved by money alone. Both at home and in the East the English organization was inferior to the Dutch. The original weakness in the constitution of the London Company still rendered it unfit for great or permanent efforts. The " separate" voyages of 1601 to 1612 had indeed given place to recurring joint stocks. But the change only superseded temporary groups of adventurers for single voyages by somewhat less temporary groups of adventurers for three or four voyages. Each group, whether for a single voyage, or for three or four, knew that its existence was limited to a brief term of years. Its object was to make as much money as it could within the period allotted to it, and to spend as little as possible on fortifications which it would have to leave behind in the East and make over at a low valuation to the next group of adventurers. The Dutch East India Company felt its interests to be bound up with those of the Dutch Government, adopted the state policy, and willingly spent vast sums on troops and fortresses in the confidence that it would reap the permanent fruits of its territorial conquests.

The English Company, in fact, still remained a private venture; the Dutch Company knew itself to be a national enterprise. The difference received emphasis from the personal character of King James. The London Company's charter was never quite safe from court intrigues. If royal favourites could no longer procure a license for English interlopers, his Majesty was King of Scotland as well as of England, and the charter did not affect his northern subjects. In the crisis of its struggle with the Dutch, the London Company learned with dismay that the king had in 1617 granted a patent to Sir James Cuningham for a Scottish Company to trade to Greenland, Muscovy, and the East Indies—

"in as ample manner and as the Company of London do."

The danger was grave. For the Scotch would not only prove keen rivals in trade, but their charter might be covertly utilized by English interlopers, and a Presbyterian nation was not unlikely to come to an understanding with the Calvinist and Lutheran Dutch. The movement which resulted in the Scottish Brigade in Holland had set in; and the London Company might find itself beset by a Scotch and Dutch combination in the East. We shall find that the steward of the Dutch factory at Amboyna in 1623 was an Aberdeen man. King James listened to the remonstrances of his English subjects, and in 1618 the new grant was recalled upon the London Company agreeing to compensate the Scotch patentee.

The concession did not come too soon. In the autumn of the same year, 1618, the English Company found itself once more compelled to appeal for state support in what now clearly revealed itself as a struggle between the Dutch and the English nations. It presented memorials to the king and the Privy Council, setting forth "the manifest and insupportable wrongs and abuses done by the Hollanders unto your Majesty and your Majesty's subjects in the East Indies." The two nutmeg islets of Pularoon and Rosengyn, with a chief town in Lantor or Great Banda which had freely surrendered to his Majesty, had been threatened or attacked by the Hollanders, and English prisoners had been publicly shown in chains. "Lo, these are the men," said the Dutch to the islanders, "whom ye made your gods, in whom ye put your trust, but we have made them our slaves." Twenty of the miserable captives were since dead of cruel usage.

The Dutch had also taken two English ships, rifled another, and put the crews in irons, declaring they had the authority of King James himself to capture any

COURT OF PROPRIETORS, EAST INDIA HOUSE.

English vessel to the east of the Celebes. They refused to restore a vessel unless we gave up our claim to Pularoon, boasting "that one Holland ship would take ten English: that they care not for our king, for Saint George was now turned child."

King James reopened negotiations in earnest (September, 1618) and demanded that Dutch commissioners should be sent to London. A report was allowed to reach The Hague that he had ordered the seizure in England of certain Dutch East Indiamen, and in November the Dutch commissioners were accredited—six on behalf of the Dutch East India Company, and four on behalf of the States-General with the Dutch ambassador at their head.

The two questions to be settled were compensation for past injuries and a fair arrangement for the future. The Dutch commissioners proved able diplomatists, "very subtle and cunning" as they seemed to our plain city men. At the very first meeting they took up a firm stand against "reparation of damage," and by January 27, 1619, they were sending for men-of-war to carry them home. When Lord Digby patched up the breach, things again came to a stand in April, as the Hollanders, while demanding that the English Company should share the charges of the Dutch fortresses in the East, refused to allow it any share in their control. The king himself now intervened, declaring that "in a matter that so nearly and highly concerns the weal of both countries, his Majesty will neither spare any travail to effect it, nor be in anything more partial to either side than if they were both his own subjects."

The king's eagerness constrained the London Company to come to terms. In July, 1619, was concluded a treaty which yielded the main points to the Hollanders and proved from the first unworkable by the English. The London Company obtained no compensation for past injuries, reckoned at £100,000 during a single year, and no share in the control of the Dutch fortifications to whose cost they were to contribute. The treaty, after granting an amnesty for all excesses on either side, and providing for a mutual restitution of ships and property, declared the trade in the East to be open to both Companies. Both Companies should exert themselves to reduce the native dues and exactions, to keep down prices of Indian commodities in

GOLD LACE WORKERS AT LUCKNOW.

the East, and to maintain a high scale of prices in Europe. On the southeast Indian coast the English were to have free trade at Pulicat on paying half the expenses of the Dutch garrison. In Java the pepper trade should be equally divided. In the Moluccas and the Banda and Amboyna Archipelagoes, which included the clove and nutmeg islands, the English should have one-third and the Dutch two-thirds of the trade, paying for the garrisons in a corresponding ratio. Each Company was to furnish ten ships of war to be kept in the East for purposes of common defence, and not to be employed on home voyages, but only in the port-to-port trade. All forts should remain in the hands of their present possessors—which practically meant of the Dutch, as we had then so few—and certain proposed fortifications of the English were to be postponed for two or three years, until both Companies could agree upon them.

The treaty was to be binding for twenty years. Its execution was to be supervised by a joint Council of Defence in the Indies, composed of four members from each Company, with an appeal in case of dispute to the States-General and the King of England. So much eventually turned on this Council of Defence clause that I give it in full.[1] Its functions were defined as the direction of the common defence by sea, the distribution of the ships of war, and the regulation of dues or imposts for maintaining the forts and garrisons.

[1] Rymer's *Fœdera* (ed. 1704–1735), vol. xvii, pp. 172–173: "Pour avec ordre establir & mieux administer ceste Defense, il sera erige un conseil de Defense compose de huict Personnes des premiers & principaux officiers, estans par dela; les quelles seront prises & eslues en nombre egal tant de l'une que de l'autre compagnie, & presideront par tour.

"Ce Conseil ordonnera de ce qui concernera le faict de la Defense commune par Mer, & distribuera les Navires de Guerre en telz endroits qu'il trouvera necessaire. Comme aussy il reiglera les Daces & Impositions qui seront necessaires pour le entretennement des dits Forts & garnisons d'iceux, & sera authorise de faire rendre compte aux Recepueurs des dites Impositions . . .

"Ce Traicte sera pour le temps de vingt ans; & sy, pendant ce temps la, arrive quelques Disputes qui ne puissent estre terminees par le dit conseil en ces Quartiers la, ny par deca par les deux compagnies, le Different en sera remis au Roy de la Grande Bretagne & aus dits seigneurs Estats Generaux, qui daigneront preindre la Peine de l'accomoder au contentement des uns & des autres."

There is no mention of civil or criminal jurisdiction, nor of any system of law to be administered.

The English Company felt that the royal rôle of peacemaker had been played chiefly at their cost. They petitioned the king in particular against the articles touching the forts, " as utterly cutting off the Company from all hope and expectation of their obtaining any parts of the forts at any time hereafter, which in the end would utterly exclude the Company from the whole trade of the Indies." Even the king's ambassador at The Hague thought the fortress clauses might have been more advantageous to us, while his friend Chamberlain plainly wrote to him: " Say what they can, things are passed as the other [side] would have it." Secretary Calvert regarded the treaty as a mere suspension of the dispute, and believed a great opportunity had been lost, for the Portuguese, French, and Danes were all eager for a trade alliance with us in the East. However, on July 16, 1619, King James ratified the engagement, and sweetened the pill to his subjects by a clause promising to erect no other East India Company during the treaty term of twenty years.

As a matter of fact, it but little affected events in the East. The treaty did not reach India till March, 1620, when the Dutch and English generals suspended their hostilities, proclaimed it on every ship from the mainmast, feasted each other, and liberated all prisoners on both sides. But their quarrel had got beyond control from home, and their amity ended as the smoke of their salvos cleared off. The English were trying to enforce two distinct claims which the Dutch believed to be incompatible with their position in the Eastern Archipelago: a claim to trade in the nutmeg and clove islands of the Banda and Amboyna groups, and a claim to a fortified settlement close to the Dutch headquarters in Java.

A glance at the map will show the significance of these claims. At the eastern end of the Archipelago lie two groups, represented for our present purpose by Amboyna, a clove island, and by the Banda, literally the "United," nutmeg isles, including Lantor or Great Banda, Pularoon, Pulaway, and Rosengyn.[1] Not only did these islets produce the most valuable spices, but they might be approached from the southwest. If the English could establish themselves in Amboyna, Pularoon, and Rosengyn, they would, so to speak, turn the flank of the Dutch positions commanding the Straits of Malacca and of Sunda. By keeping to the south of the line of long islands (Sumatra, Java, Flores, Timor, etc.) they could secure a direct access, not unattended indeed by nautical dangers, to the clove and nutmeg archipelago. These matters, which were hidden from King James and his councillors, were vital to the Dutch control of the spice trade. The Dutch directors in Holland understood them better; and while granting us

[1] Amboyna is an islet 32 miles long with an area of about 280 square miles, to the south of the larger island of Ceram, which is itself one of the southernmost of the Moluccas or Spice Islands. The Banda group lies still further south than Amboyna, but Pularoon and Pulaway, although prominent in the struggle between the Dutch and English, are so small as not to be shown on ordinary maps. They are not mentioned even in Vivien de St. Martin's great Dictionary of Geography (Paris, 1879).

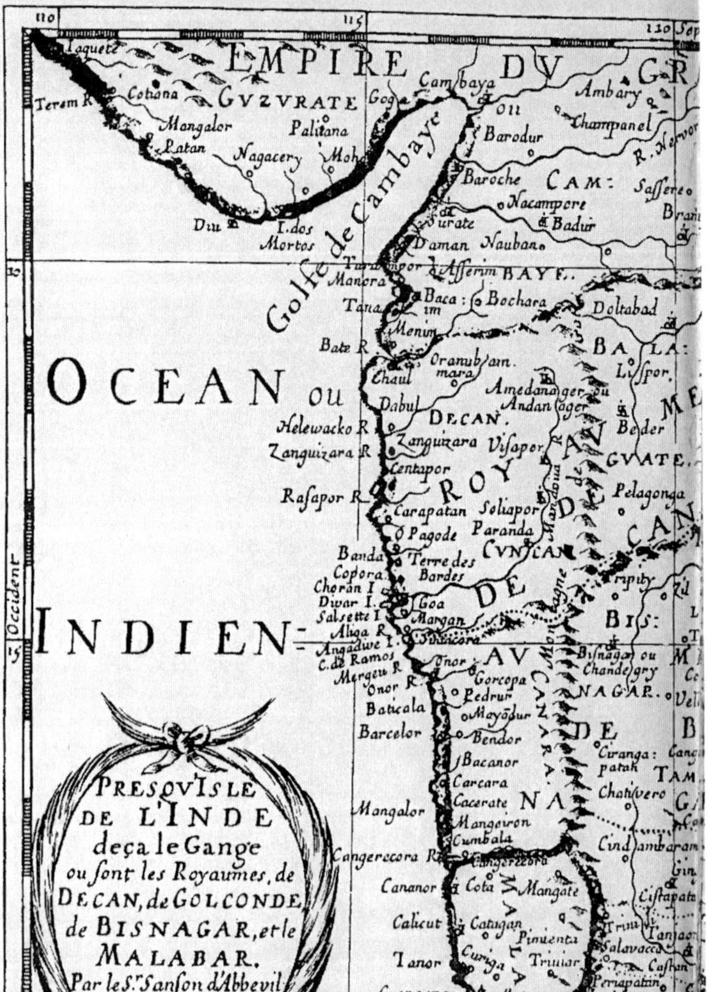

A Seventeenth-ce

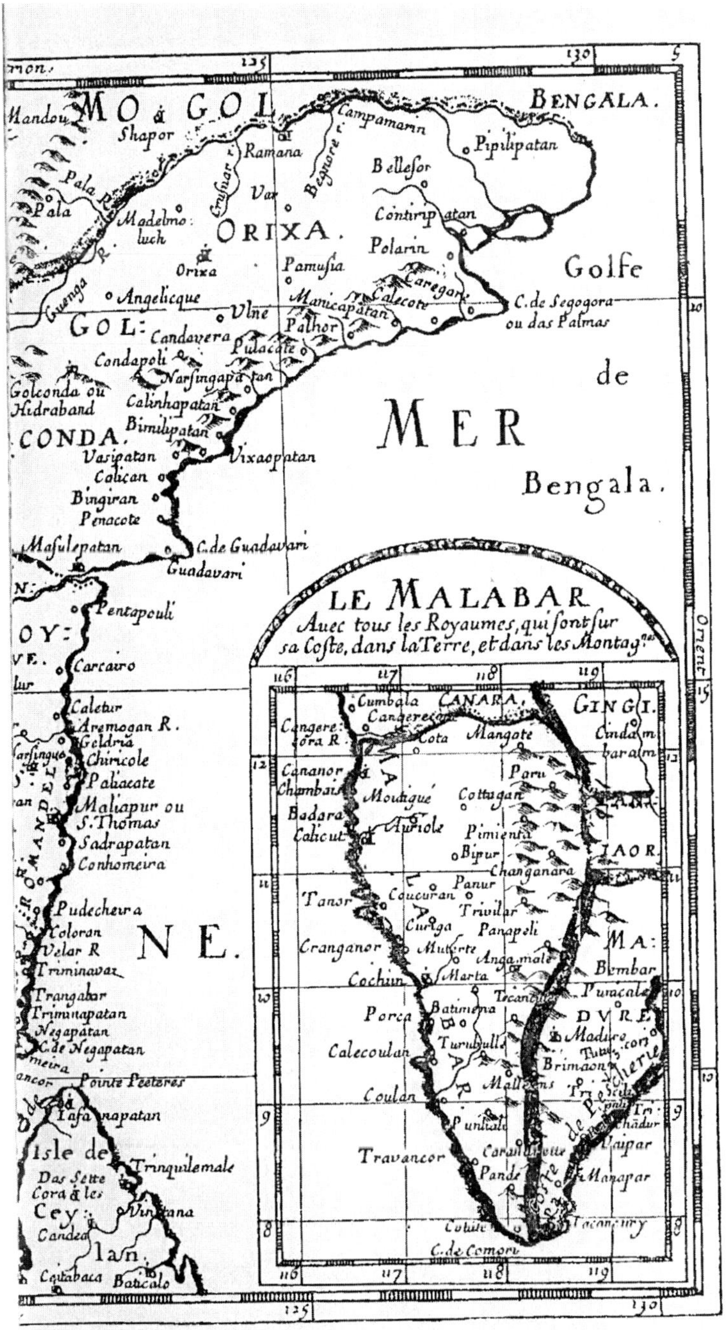

y Map of India.

an equal share in the cheap pepper of Java, they would concede only one-third of the traffic with the clove and nutmeg islands of the further East. We were outmatched in point of knowledge as in armed force.

The Dutch rested their title to these islands on their conquest from the Portuguese and on treaties with the local chiefs. The English claimed that they were places of common resort for the spice trade, that in some of them they had built blockhouses which the Dutch pulled down, and that others, including Amboyna, Pularoon, and Rosengyn, had granted us a settlement or freely placed themselves under the protection of King James. The struggle for them, with its mutual outrages and reprisals, need not be detailed. It commenced as far back as 1608, became acute after 1616, and ended with the catastrophe of Amboyna in 1623.

While the English tried to circumvent the Dutch western positions on the Malacca and Sunda straits, and to fasten on the richest spice isles of the easternmost archipelago, they also threatened the Dutch settlements in Java itself. In December, 1618, the English by way of reprisal captured the Dutch *Black Lion* at Bantam. In January, 1619, they beat the Dutch fleet in a "cruel bloody fight" in which three thousand great shot were fired without lasting result, and in October the Dutch defeated our squadron off Sumatra —the last battle for the famous old *Red Dragon*. The Dutch *Black Lion* had a less noble end—being accidentally burned while in our possession by four drunken English sailors, one of whom we hanged and the other three were flogged round the fleet.

This sea-struggle around the western entrances into the Archipelago had its counterpart conflict on shore. The ships of the two Protestant nations were individually pretty well matched, the captains equally skilful, the crews equally brave, and victory sometimes fell to the one, sometimes to the other. Our cursing and stamping admiral, Sir Thomas Dale—a determined man, bred in the cruel school of the Spanish-Dutch war—had by unsparing severity wrung order out of anarchy in Virginia, and was sent with six ships to India in 1618. But the English found the land forces in Java numerically superior to their own, and directed by a man of still more masterful character, and with a genius for organization not possessed by any other European then in the East.

A NATIVE OF JAVA.

Jan Pieterszoon Coen, born at Hoorn in 1587, had learned the secrets of commerce in the famous house of the Piscatori at Rome, and went first to Dutch India in 1607. By 1613 his talents raised him to the office of director-general of commerce and president at Bantam, with the control of all outlying agencies (*comp-*

toirs). In 1617 the Council of Seventeen appointed him governor-general, with a ratification from the States-General and a commission direct from Prince Maurice of Orange—powers so ample as afterwards to warrant him in questioning orders of the directors unless approved of by the States-General. In June, 1618, he entered on his high office at Java. "If the King of England does not make it his particular care," a shrewd French observer reported, "the English run the risk of having the worst in the Indies, as being weaker than the Flemings are in that country."

Coen was to the Dutch Indies in the seventeenth century what Albuquerque had been to the Portuguese in the sixteenth, and what Dupleix became to the French in the eighteenth. He resolved to found the Dutch power on a lasting territorial basis. His clear vision of a Dutch empire in the East met with opposition from narrower minds—the antagonism which Albuquerque's policy had encountered from the honest Almeida, and which the schemes of Dupleix were to receive from a corrupt French court. But the Dutch Company, like the English Company in after days, knew a great man when they got one; and in spite of internal differences and a temporary eclipse, Coen was supported, rewarded, and honoured. His two governor-generalships, from 1618 to 1623, and from 1627 to 1629, form the seed-time of the Dutch greatness in the East.

A strongly fortified capital, commanding the western entrance to the Archipelago, yet centrally situated, was necessary to his design. The Straits of Malacca were already controlled by treaties, and circumstances led Coen to the northern exit of the Straits of Sunda as the position from which to dominate the island world. The two possible sites were Bantam and Jacatra at the northwestern end of Java, where the Sunda Straits debouch into the Archipelago. Bantam was nearer to the straits, Jacatra lay round the corner to the northeast, but was the stronger position. Both places were resorted to by the English and Dutch, and the two nations claimed treaty rights with the native princes at each. One of Coen's first acts as governor-general was to obtain leave from the Jacatra chief for a fortified settlement on his river.

Presently the Jacatra and Bantam chiefs grew afraid of the rising fortress, and, although not liking the English, obtained their help to expel the Dutch. Coen had sailed to the Moluccas to avenge a native revolt and to reunite his fleet; and in January-February, 1619, the Dutch at Jacatra, after a defence of their half-built walls, had to capitulate. They agreed to surrender their fortress, people, and war munitions to the English, and the money and goods of the Dutch Company to the native prince. The English were to provide a ship to convey away the Hollanders to the Indian coast of Coromandel, or whithersoever they might resolve to go, except to the Moluccas or Amboyna.

The claims of Bantam caused delay, and Coen had now reunited his fleet at the Moluccas. His return

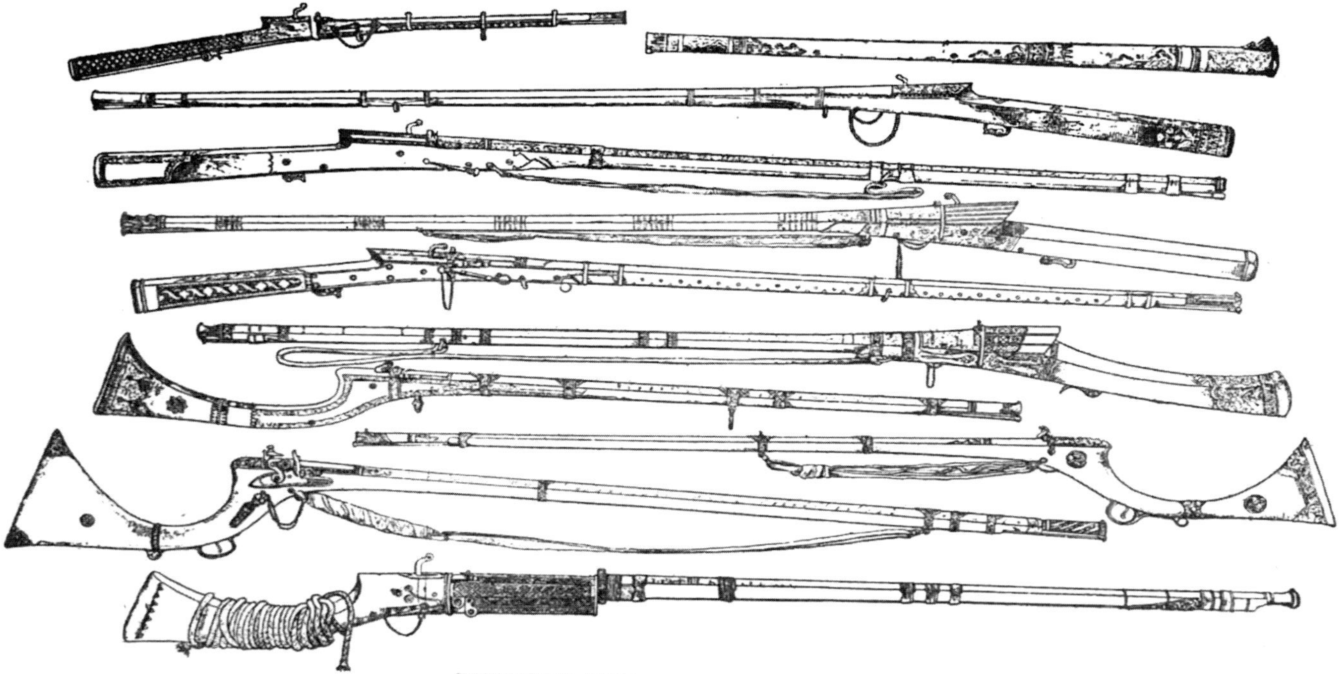

MATCHLOCKS FROM VARIOUS PARTS OF INDIA.

to Java prevented the treaty from being carried out. In the spring of 1619 he utterly destroyed the native town of Jacatra, seized the estuary of the river together with the adjacent territory, and built on it the city and fortress from which, under the new name of Batavia, the Dutch rule the Eastern Archipelago to this day.

Our admiral, brave, passionate Dale, having unwisely divided his fleet, and being stricken with fever from the swamps of the Jacatra River, sailed for India. Coen hurried on the fortifications at Batavia so as to give the complete command of the Jacatra estuary to the Dutch. He prepared to punish the Bantam prince who had joined and then quarrelled with the English during his (Coen's) absence in the Moluccas. He drew the bonds tighter on the English trade, and resolved to use our alliance with Bantam as a *casus belli* for driving us out of the Spice Islands. At this juncture, early in 1620, the Anglo-Dutch treaty of July, 1619, arrived at Batavia, with its amnesty for the past and promise of peace in the future.

But scarcely had the joint cheering for King James and Prince Maurice died away and the fleets been stripped of their bunting, than the treaty of 1619 was discerned to be itself a new source of strife. In 1618 the Dutch directors frankly wrote to Coen that, although they were trying to come to an agreement with the London Company, yet in the meanwhile he was "strictly to carry out our previous orders for expelling the English and all other nations from all treaty places or where we have forts." Coen had laid his plans accordingly. The Dutch directors were, however, willing to give the treaty of 1619 a fair chance. "It is our sincere and earnest desire," they wrote in 1619-1620, honestly to observe its terms, and they even con-

CAPE TOWN AND TABLE MOUNTAIN.
(Copyright by Underwood and Underwood, New York.)

templated building a fortress at the Cape of Good Hope jointly with the English. But they insisted on our executing our engagements to the utmost letter, and above all on our maintaining the full complement of war-ships agreed on.

The last condition was one which the English Company could not fulfil. Coen knew this and foresaw that its nonfulfilment would leave him a free hand. While he therefore made fair arrangements for the joint Council of Defence on shore, for the mutual command of the fleet, and for carrying the two national flags at the mainmast every alternate fortnight, a guarded or even hostile attitude to the English was enjoined on the outlying Dutch settlements.

The truth is the two Companies had widely different interests in the main business of defence. The Dutch truce with Spain was about to expire (1621), and Holland resolved to break the Spanish-Portuguese power in the East as a preparation for the inevitable European war. The English were by no means so anxious to attack the Spaniards, with whom they were ostensibly at peace, and whom they believed they could undersell in an open market by the fair rivalry of trade. After several joint expeditions, the English failed to supply their quota of ships, but offered to pay half the naval expenses. Then they withdrew more openly, and after bitter recriminations the Dutch declared that the English "have neither law nor justice . . . the knife of the one [alone] keeps the knife of the other in the sheath." The English replied that the Dutch used the alliance for their own ends, and that the treaty was for a fleet of defence and not for conquest. In 1623 they declined to join in a third expedition against the Spanish Manilas and their ships separated from the Dutch alike in Java and the Moluccas.

A second cause of quarrel arose out of the blockade of Bantam, which the joint council undertook, but which the English soon declared to be a plan of conquest outside the duties of "defence." The English only wanted an open trade at Bantam, and this the prince was willing to concede. The Dutch desired to avenge the attack of Bantam on their rising fort at Jacatra in 1618, and to ruin the trade of a rival port lying so close to their new Batavian capital. The question of the sovereign jurisdiction in the Archipelago supplied a third and more bitter subject of strife. The Dutch directors explicitly ordered that the laws of Holland were to be observed at Batavia; that the claim given by the treaty to the English was to a share of the trade but to no share of the *dominium*; and that the treaty had not "reduced our rights even in the smallest way in the Moluccas, Amboyna, and Banda." The treaty had, in fact, omitted to provide for the question of jurisdiction. The English president himself was fined in 1621 for not obeying orders issued at Batavia in the name of the States-General, and in 1622 he was mulcted on the complaint of a native.

A fourth cause of quarrel was the money contribution for fortifications under the treaty. Here again the two nations had opposed interests in the East. It was the Flemish policy of ruining Spain by armed trade, as against the London Company's desire for open ports. The Dutch wanted as many fortifications as they could get at the joint expense; the English wanted few fortifications, and none which they could not control. The

The Residency at Lucknow

The British Residency at Lucknow became famous because of its connection with the momentous events in the struggle for supremacy between Orient and Occident in India during the Mutiny of 1857.

Dutch accused the English of insufficient subsidies. The English replied that, while they found the money, the Dutch spent it, or pocketed it, as they pleased, and made no equal contribution on their part. The Dutch records themselves disclose some laxity in this respect. In 1621 the Dutch cut down the outlay on forts, garrisons, and the governor's table allowances, yet warned their agents that "the English need not get the benefit of it," but are to be charged as before. Nor were the English to be allowed to "build or make anything at their own expense, on which hereafter they can claim ownership." All this is clear from Dutch manuscript records in the India Office. The English retaliated for the imposts enforced from them for fortresses in the Eastern Archipelago, by levying dues from Flemish ships near Ormuz, to the wrath of the Dutch captains.

The restitution of property clause furnished a fifth ground of wrangling, in which both sides thought themselves overreached. The constant and bitter personal disputes between the local agents of the two Companies supplied a sixth cause, which would alone have rendered unworkable the treaty of 1619. Within two years King James himself recognized that it had broken down. In March, 1621, he pressed the Dutch Government to send commissioners again, and in July he hastened its decision by threatening letters of marque. The commissioners arrived in England in November, 1621, but their negotiations were spun out to January, 1623—too late to avert the impending tragedy.

As Barneveldt's project for a United Dutch-English

Company had been strangled by the diplomatic discord at London and The Hague, so all hope of compromise between the two nations was stifled amid the passionate disputes of their sea-captains in the East, and extinguished for ever in the torture chamber of Amboyna.

DECORATION FROM AN INDIAN SWORD.

CHAPTER IV

THE END OF THE STRUGGLE: THE TRAGEDY OF AMBOYNA

1623

EVENTS were now hastening to a catastrophe. The Dutch governor-general, Coen, while resolved to make the Archipelago an island empire for Holland, was too sagacious to imperil his plans by putting his nation openly in the wrong toward a great European power. He trusted to the treaty of 1619 itself to afford causes of quarrel, which would enable him to carry out the instructions given to the first Dutch governor-general, 1609 - 1614, and steadily reiterated ever since, that "the commerce of the Moluccas, Amboyna, and Banda should belong to the Company, and that no other nation in the world should possess the least part." But Coen's far-reaching policy was beyond the grasp of his bluff ship-captains, with their flaming broadsides, or of the angry isolated Dutch agents, a thousand miles apart, with their forts and prison cells.

Coen himself believed that the treaty alone stood in the way of his triumph over the English. Our Admiral Dale, stricken with fever, and fearful lest the Bantamese might sacrifice the English to make terms with the Dutch, had shipped off our goods and factors from Bantam in the summer of 1619, sought an asylum for them on the east coast of India, and there died. The English ships that remained in the Archipelago seemed destined to fall to the Dutch, who captured two of them in July, 1619, and four others off Sumatra in October. Our alliance with the Prince of Bantam, to capture the half-built Dutch fort at Jacatra (Batavia) in the beginning of that year, furnished Coen with a cause of war against us, and placed him in the right from the point of view of European diplomacy. The arrival, early in 1620, of the treaty of July, 1619, snatched the prey from between his hands. "The English ought to be very thankful to you," he wrote to the Dutch directors in Holland, "for they had worked themselves very nicely out of the Indies, and you have placed them again in the midst."

If, however, he had to obey the treaty, he could use it for his own ends. The English would have liked to resettle at Bantam, but Coen resolved not only to destroy the trade of that port but to force the English to live under his own eye at Batavia. After some negotiation the joint Council of Defence, established in Java by the treaty, agreed to blockade Bantam in 1620, and thus accomplished both his objects. For, although the English soon withdrew, they had compromised themselves with the Bantam prince, and the Dutch fleet was strong enough to continue the blockade without them.

COURT OF DIRECTORS, EAST INDIA HOUSE.

In Batavia Coen made our position so miserable that in July, 1620, we had to keep a ship there as a floating warehouse, "having no place on shore." In 1621 the English almost gave up Java in despair, and part of them again sought a refuge on the Indian coast. In August, 1622, Thomas Drockedon, our agent at Batavia, asked leave from the directors in London to return home, as he could "live no longer under the insolence of the Dutch."

His situation was a mournful one. So far from restitution having been made to us under the treaty of 1619, we were compelled to supply "incredible sums" for fortifications which the Dutch did or did not build, but which could only be a menace to ourselves. We had been dragged into a war with Bantam, from which we could derive no benefit, and which shut us out from the chief pepper mart. The civil and criminal jurisdiction was exercised by the Dutch to publicly insult us. We were placed on a level with "the blacks," whose bare affirmation was taken against us. We might not "kill a wild hog or gather a cocoanut in the wood without leave." The Dutch had flogged William Clarke, steward of the English factory, in the market-place, "cruelly cutting his flesh, and then washed him with salt and vinegar, and laid him again in irons." The English watch had been imprisoned for eight days and threatened with torture, to force them to make false confessions against the president of our council. What seemed to the Dutch their lawful jurisdiction, the English regarded as oppression.

For another alleged plot twelve natives had been condemned to be quartered, and the rest of the accused to perpetual slavery in chains. The torture failed to elicit anything against the English; but if it could have given the Dutch "any advantage against us," we should have had no mercy. "Wherefore," wrote in 1622 our President Fursland and council at Batavia, "we earnestly desire speedily to be released from this bondage." A similar attempt was made in the island of Pularoon to extort confessions against the English by cruel torments of the natives. Thus was rehearsed alike in the capital of Dutch India and in the distant Nutmeg Isles, that tragedy of torture which was so soon to be enacted at Amboyna. In the still remoter seas, as we learn from a letter of Richard Cocks, dated Nagasaki, 10th March, 1620, the Hollanders, with seven ships at Japan, had, "with sound of trumpet," "proclaimed there open war against the English, as their mortal enemies."

The Clove and Nutmeg Isles, including among them Amboyna, Banda, and Pularoon, lay, it will be remembered, at the southeastern end of the Spice Archipelago. The Dutch claimed the sovereignty over them, by the conquest of Amboyna from the Portuguese in 1605, and in virtue of many treaties. The English had a set of counter-claims based on the free surrender of Pularoon to us in 1616, of Lantor or Great Banda in 1620, and on compacts with other chiefs. We had also an agency at Amboyna under the Dutch-English treaty of 1619. The Dutch with an overwhelming force expelled us from Lantor and Pularoon in 1621-1622. Our gallant agent, Nathaniel Courthorpe, who, in "much want and misery," held Pularoon from 1616 to 1620, sometimes with but thirty-eight men to resist the "force and tyranny" of the Hollanders, had been mortally wounded in a sea-fight, and threw himself overboard rather than see his ship strike her flag.

Herman van Speult, governor of the neighbouring island of Amboyna, was regarded at headquarters as "too scrupulous" in his fiscal administration. In January, 1623, the Governor-General Coen, when departing for Europe, enjoined strict justice, and mentioned Amboyna as a place where no English encroachments were to be allowed. "Trust them not," he said, "any more than open enemies . . . not weighing too scrupulously what may fall out." His farewell instructions merely reiterated the principles on which he had always insisted. "Trust the English no more than a public enemy ought to be trusted," he wrote two months previously to Banda, the agency nearest Amboyna. This policy of suspicion, and of "not weighing too scrupulously what may fall out," was now to be enforced with a stupid violence which the great governor-general might perhaps have anticipated, but which he would have been the first to condemn.

By the beginning of 1623 the Dutch found themselves completely masters of the Clove and Nutmeg Archipelago. At the principal clove island, Amboyna, they had, according to the English statement founded upon depositions on oath, a fortress garrisoned by two hundred Dutch soldiers, with three or four hundred native troops, including some thirty Japanese, and further protected by eight vessels in the roadstead. The English numbered eighteen men, scattered between five small factories on different islands, very badly off, with a few slaves, "just six and all boys." In their house at Amboyna only three swords, two muskets, and half a pound of powder were found. The nearest English support was the Banda agency, at a distance across the sea, and containing but nine of their countrymen. English ships seldom came to Amboyna, and not one was then near. Our president in council at Java had in fact resolved to withdraw the petty English factories at Amboyna and throughout the Clove and Nut-

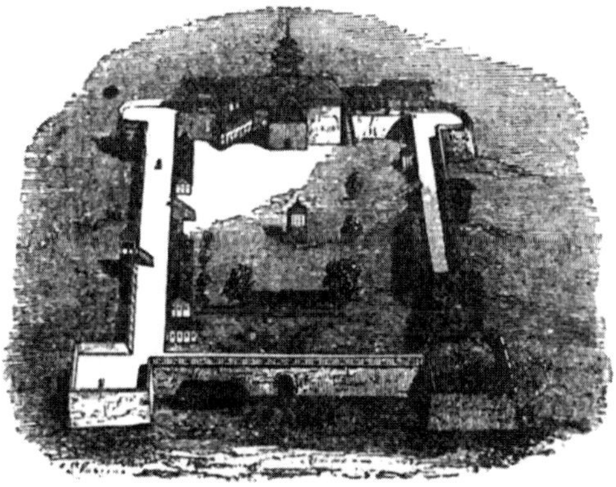

THE FORTRESS AT AMBOYNA.

meg Archipelago. He had even arranged with the Dutch governor-general for their transport to Batavia in Holland ships. In February, 1623, orders to this effect were on their way from our president in Batavia to Amboyna.

They arrived too late. On the evening of February 10, 1623, a Japanese soldier of the Dutch garrison had some talk with the sentries about the number of the troops and the times of changing the watch. When questioned by the Governor Van Speult next day, February 11th, he explained that he had merely chatted with the soldiers "for his own amusement." Indeed, the steward of the Dutch factory afterwards declared that "it was an usual speech amongst soldiers to enquire one of another how strong the watch might be, that they might know how many hours they might stand sentinel."

Van Speult was, however, on the lookout for conspiracy, and perhaps anxious to redeem his reputation from the charge of slackness at headquarters. In the previous summer he had written to the Governor-General Coen about the English at Amboyna: "We hope to direct things according to your orders that our sovereignty shall not be diminished or injured in any way by their encroachments, and if we may hear of any conspiracies of theirs against the sovereignty, we shall with your sanction do justice to them, suitably, unhesitatingly, and immediately." In October, 1622, Coen gave this sanction. In February, 1623, the opportunity arrived. Van Speult put the Japanese soldier to the torture, and after he had "endured pretty long," wrung from him an accusation against the English. His statement was signed by the unhappy man on the day of his torment, in direct contravention of the Dutch law that one who had confessed under torture should be re-heard to confirm it not sooner than twenty-four hours afterwards, "*ne durare adhuc tormentorum metus videàtur.*"

Eight or nine other Japanese soldiers in the service of the Dutch, whose names he had mentioned, denied the plot, but were tortured on that and the following day, until a complete story of treason was evolved.

"Wailing and weeping by reason of their extreme tortures with burning, they were carried by slaves to prison, for it was not possible of themselves to go on their feet." Such was the statement made by the steward of the Dutch factory regarding the affair.

The handful of English, ran the improbable tale, had solemnly sworn on New Year's Day to seize the fort upon the arrival of an English ship, or during the absence of the Dutch governor, and had employed to corrupt the Japanese soldiers so unlikely an agent as a drunken barber, or barber-surgeon, Abel Price. This man already lay in the Dutch prison for threatening to set fire to a house in a frenzy of liquor. On February 15th, as the records show, he, too, was haled to the torture-chamber, and made to "confess whatever they asked him."

A SHIP OF THE SEVENTEENTH CENTURY.
After a contemporary print.

The English treated as ridiculous the story that eighteen men, scattered over the two islands of Amboyna and Ceram, at the factories of Amboyna, Hittou, Larica, Loho, and Cambello, should dare conspire to take a fort from two hundred Dutch and three or four hundred native soldiers with eight Holland vessels in the harbour, and they went about their business as usual. But Van Speult, now armed with the confession under torture of his prisoner, the drunken English barber, seized our chief agent, Towerson, and the other factors at Amboyna, put them in irons, and swept in the whole English from the four outlying factories between February 15th and 23d—just eighteen men all told.

Of the extraordinary proceedings that followed we have six accounts by eye-witnesses. First, the minutes of the court, kept by the Greffier or secretary: minutes so irregular and incomplete as to call forth the censure of the Dutch governor-general, and to invalidate them as a judicial record under the Dutch law. Second, the solemn dying messages of the victims written on the pages of their prayer-books or other furtive scraps of paper. Third, the statements of certain members of the Dutch Council at Amboyna who formed the court, when called to account by the governor-general at Batavia two and a half years later (October, 1625). These latter admit the use of torture, passed over in silence by the minutes, but state that it was slight. Fourth, the depositions of six Englishmen who survived, taken on oath before Sir Henry Marten, Judge of the Admiralty, in 1624. Fifth, the answers of certain of the Amboyna judges to interrogatories in 1628. Sixth, the statement of the steward of the Dutch factory, who also acted as interpreter during the trial. It was laid before Lord Dorchester and Secretary Coke in 1629. This man, George Forbis or Forbisher, a native of Aberdeen, and little likely to favour the English Company which persuaded James to cancel the charter granted to the Scotch, had long served the Dutch in the East, and was found on board a Dutch ship stayed by royal command at Portsmouth in 1627. He had continued in the Dutch service for two years after the trial. His declaration closely corresponds with the depositions of the English survivors.

In my narrative I fairly consider all the foregoing materials, together with the pamphlet literature which quickly sprang up.[1] I have also checked the "True Relation" from the depositions on oath.

That evidence consisted entirely of confessions wrung from the accused by torture. The ransacking of the English factories yielded not a single incriminating letter, or other corroborative piece of testimony, as is proved by the answer of Joosten, the Dutch officer who examined the papers. The Dutch began with John Beaumont and Timothy Johnson. Beaumont, an elderly man for India and an invalid, was left with a guard in the hall, while Johnson was taken into another room. Presently Beaumont heard him "cry out very pitifully;

[1] The chief contemporary pamphlets on the Amboyna tragedy are six in number.

(i) *A True Relation of the Unjust, Cruel, and Barbarous Proceedings against the English at Amboyna.* This narrative was "taken out of the depositions of six several English factors" who survived the trial, as delivered on oath before Sir Henry Marten, Judge of the Admiralty, supplemented by the testimony of Welden, the English chief agent in Banda at the time of the tragedy. The Privy Council in September, 1624, gave their opinion that the relation was justified by the statements of the six witnesses. *Calendar of State Papers*, East Indies, 1622–1624, par. 620.

(ii) *A True Declaration of the Newes that came out of the East Indies, with the Pinace called the "Hare."* A Dutch pamphlet which appeared anonymously, and was thought by some to be the work of Boreel. The Directors of the Dutch Company denied the authorship, and, on complaint of the English ambassador, the States-General issued a proclamation declaring it to be "a scandalous and then be quiet for a little while, and then loud again." Johnson long refused to confess, but after an hour he was "brought forth wailing and lamenting, all wet and cruelly burnt in divers parts of his body."

One Englishman, Edward Collins, gave evidence, according to the Dutch, without torture. But the narrative founded upon the depositions of the surviving Englishmen on oath states that Collins was tied up for the torture, and the cloth put about his throat. "Thus prepared he prayed to be respited and he would confess all. Being let down he again vowed and protested his innocency," but for fear of the torture asked them what he should say. This was not enough and he was tortured, but not being able to endure it long, he made a confession helped out by the Dutch prosecutor. Collins himself confirmed this statement on oath and produced three witnesses who "heard him many times roar very pitifully, being in the next room, and saw

senseless libel," and offering a reward of 400 guilders for the discovery of either the author or the printer.

(iii) *An Answer to the Dutch Relation touching the pretended Conspiracy of the English at Amboyna in the Indies*, being a reply to No. ii. (the libellous Dutch *Declaration*) drawn up by the English Company and issued under its authority. These three pamphlets were published together by the Company in 1624 with a preface. A third reprint is dated 1632, and there were several subsequent editions.

(iv) *A Remonstrance of the Directors of the Netherlands East India Company presented to the Lords States-General . . . in defence of the said Company touching the bloody Proceedings against the English Merchants executed at Amboyna.*

(v) *The Acts of the Council of Amboyna.* The official Court Record of the Trial and the confessions of the accused, as presented by the Dutch to the East India Company.

(vi) *A Reply to the Defence of the Proceedings of the Dutch against the English at Amboyna.* An answer to, and criticism of, Nos. iv. and v. These last three pamphlets were published by authority in London in 1632.

him come out, having no doublet on, his shirt all wet, his face swollen and his eyes starting out of his head."

From February 15th to 23d the cruel process went on. According to the English statements, the prisoners, even while confessing under the torture, declared in the same breath that they were not speaking truth. In the case of Collins, the "fiscal," or prosecutor, forced leading questions upon him, till one of the Dutch themselves exclaimed: "Do not tell him what he should say, but let him speak for himself." John Wetheral having been four times tied up, they were at length obliged to read out to him the confessions of the other victims until the poor wretch merely "answered yea to all." He "prayed them to tell him what he should say or to write down what they would; he would subscribe it." John Clarke stood the ordeal so bravely that "the tormentors reviled him, saying that he was a devil . . . or a witch." So they "cut off his hair very short, as supposing he had some witchcraft hidden therein." They then went on with the torture—burning him with candles on the feet, hands, elbows, and "under the armpits until his inwards might evidently be seen." The English declared that no surgeon was allowed to dress the sores "until, his flesh being putrefied, great maggots dropt and crept from him in most loathsome and noisome manner." Authority for all these statements may be found in the first pamphlet, "A True Relation."

According to the English accounts each confession was wrung forth by torture. The Dutch minutes of the trial conceal the fact of torture at all, and thus violate a fundamental rule of the Dutch criminal procedure. The members of the Amboyna council, who sat as judges, acknowledged on oath that twelve of the English were tortured by water and two of them also by fire, but stated that one (Beaumont) was only tortured a little on account of his age and feeble health.

AMBOYNA.

The judges also pleaded in their defence that the torture was in no case extreme, indeed of a "civil" sort.

What it exactly amounted to we know from eyewitnesses. The accused man was hoisted up and tied spread-eagle fashion in a doorway. In the water torment "they bound a cloth about his neck and face so close that little or no water could go by. That done they poured the water softly upon his head until the cloth was full up to the mouth and nostrils . . . till his body was swollen twice or thrice as big as before, his cheeks like great bladders, and his eyes staring and strutting out beyond his forehead." It was the slow agony of bursting, joined to the acute but long-drawn-out agony of suffocation. In the fire torture, they held lighted candles beneath the most sensitive parts of the body—under the armpits, the palms of the hand, and the soles of the feet. Emmanuel Thomson, like John Clarke, it was said, had no surgeon to dress his burnt flesh, so that no one "was able to endure the smell of his body."

To the torture by fire and water, admitted by the Dutch, the English accounts add "the splitting of the toes, and lancing of the breast, and putting in gun-powder, and then firing the same, whereby the body is not left entire, neither for innocency nor execution. Clarke and Thomson were both fain to be carried to their execution, though they were tortured many days before." But the Dutch admissions suffice.

Towerson, who steadily asserted his innocence, on being confronted with some who had confessed, "charged them as they would answer it at the dreadful day of judgment, they should speak nothing but the truth." The sufferers implored his forgiveness and declared all they had said was false. But, threatened again with torture, they reaffirmed their confessions. The spirit of the miserable little band was completely broken.

Even Van Speult felt that he might be going too far, and for some days hesitated as to whether he should not remit the case to the Dutch governor-general at Batavia. But the English president and council at Batavia had, on January 10-20, 1623, resolved to withdraw their oppressed factories from the Moluccas, Amboyna, and the Clove and Nutmeg Isles. They had indeed thanked the Dutch president and council for agreeing to bring them away in Flemish ships. Orders in this sense were simultaneously sent to our agents at Banda and elsewhere. The Calendar of State Papers of the East Indies for 1622-1624 (p. 398) shows that while the tortured men lay waiting their doom, two Holland ships arrived from Batavia, bringing the letter from the English president and council ordering the withdrawal of our agency from Amboyna. "Which letter was opened and read by the Dutch governor while our people were yet in prison and not executed, and might well have secured him that there was no further danger to be feared of the English aid of shipping, whatever the English had through fear of torture confessed." The statement is confirmed by Van Speult's own admissions, and it gives a darker shade to his resolve on instant judgment.

The public prosecutor was instructed to demand sentence. This, according to the minutes, he did with irregular brevity—twenty-one lines of writing in all. According to the Dutch procedure, his requisition should have given a summary of the facts and evidence, which it did not. It should certainly have specified the separate names of the accused Englishmen, while it only contained that of Gabriel Towerson "and his creatures and accomplices." These were not the omissions of ignorance. The "fiscal" who conducted the case was a lawyer, and in his haste for condemna-

A Scene at Darjiling.
From a Photograph.

tion, he set at defiance the safeguards of procedure which even the Dutch law prescribed. His demand was really the demand of Sieyes at the trial of Louis XVI —*La Mort sans phrase.*

On February 25, 1623, or February 23d (for there are discrepancies as to the date), the prisoners, with certain exceptions, were condemned to death. The English from outlying factories, who had not even been at Amboyna at the time of the alleged plot, were released; three others were allowed to draw lots for their life; and in the end the elderly Beaumont and the terrified Collins were sent to give evidence at Batavia as "men condemned and left to the mercy of the governor-general." Captain Towerson manfully proclaimed the iniquity of the proceedings. When ordered to indite a confession, he wrote out a protestation of his innocence. The governor gave it to the interpreter to read out in Dutch, "which I could not do," said that officer, "without shedding of tears." He had also to translate a dying declaration secretly written by Towerson in a Bible which he asked Van Speult to send to his friends in England—"which Bible after that time I never saw or heard mentioned."

Yet some last words reached the outer world. William Griggs wrote in his Table-book, which was secretly saved by a servant: "We through torment were constrained to speak that which we never meant nor once imagined. . . . They tortured us with that extreme torment of fire and water that flesh and blood could not endure. . . . Written in the dark." Captain Towerson wrote much, but all was suppressed, except an unnoticed sentence appended to his signature to a bill of debt due from the English Company: "Firmed by the Firm [*i. e.* signature] of me Gabriel Towerson now appointed to die, guiltless of anything that can be justly laid to my charge. God forgive them their guilt and receive me to His mercy. Amen."

THE OLD EAST INDIA HOUSE (ABOUT 1650).

Samuel Colson, imprisoned with six of the others, on board the Dutch ships in the roads, wrote the following in his prayer-book and had it sewed up in a bed: "March 5, *stilo novo*, being Sunday, aboard the *Rotterdam*, lying in irons." "Understand that I, Samuel Colson, late factor of Hitou, was apprehended for suspicion of conspiracy; and for anything I know must die for it: wherefore having no means to make my innocence known, have writ in this book hoping some good Englishman will see it. I do here upon my salvation, as I hope by His death and passion to have redemption for my sins, that I am clear of all such conspiracy; neither do I know any Englishman guilty thereof nor any other creature in the world. As this is true, God bless me, Sam. Colson." In another part of the book, at the beginning of the Psalms, he declared: "As I mean and hope to have pardon for my sins, I know no more than the child unborn of this business." These statements were written three or four days before the execution of the death sentence, as "March 5, *stilo novo*," would correspond to February 23d, if we take the English dates.

On February 26th (English date) the prisoners were brought into the hall of the castle to be prepared for death. Captain Towerson was taken into the torture-chamber with "two great jars of water carried after him. What he there did or suffered is unknown to the English without, but it seemeth they made him then to underwrite his confession"—a confession of a plot so wild that, had it ever entered a man's brain, "he should," in the words of the English Company, "rather have been sent to bedlam . . . than to the gallows."

The condemned men still protested their innocence. "Samuel Colson spake with a loud voice saying, According to my innocency in this treason, so Lord pardon all the rest of my sins; and if I be guilty thereof more or less, let me never be partaker of Thy heavenly joys. At which words every one of the rest cried Amen for me, Amen for me, good Lord. This done, each of them knowing whom he had accused, went one to another begging forgiveness for their false accusation," under the torture; "and they all freely forgave one another, for none had been so falsely accused, but he himself had accused another as falsely." Their last "doleful night they spent in prayer, singing of psalms and comforting one another," refusing the wine which the guards offered them, "bidding them to drink lustick and drive away the sorrow."

Next day, February 27th (English date), the ten Englishmen,[1] nine Japanese, and the Portuguese captain of slaves were led out to execution "in a long procession round the town," through crowds of natives who had been summoned by beat of drum "to behold this triumph over the English."

It is not needful, after the fashion of that time, to accept as manifestations of divine wrath a "great darkness" and hurricane which immediately followed, and drove two Dutch ships from their anchorage; or the pestilence, said to have swept away one thousand people. The innocence of Towerson and his fellow sufferers rests upon no such stories, whether false or true. The improbability of the enterprise, the absence of any evidence except such as was wrung forth under torments, the neglect of the safeguards imposed by the Dutch law on judicial torture, the dying declarations of the victims—suffice to convince any unbiassed mind that the ten Englishmen were unjustly done to death. This, too, without insisting on the circumstance that would place Van Speult's conduct in the darkest light—his being on the outlook for conspiracies; or on the arrival of the English letter during the trial ordering

[1] Captain Gabriel Towerson; Samuel Colson, factor at Hitto; Emanuel Thomson, assistant at Amboyna; Timothy Johnson, assistant at Amboyna; John Wetheral, factor at Cambello; John Clark, assistant at Hitto; William Griggs, factor at Larica; John Fardo, steward of the House; Abel Price (the drunken barber-surgeon); Robert Brown, tailor.

the withdrawal of our agency from Amboyna; or on the existence of Dutch ships in the harbour which might even, if the shore prison were overcrowded, have carried those accused of the supposed conspiracy for judgment to the Dutch governor-general at Batavia, or served for their confinement till his confirmation of the proceedings was obtained.

Van Speult took possession of our Amboyna and neighbouring factories; "the poor remnant of the English" were removed to Batavia; and the great design for driving us out of the Clove and Nutmeg Isles was accomplished.

When the news of the tragedy reached England fifteen months later—May 29, 1624—a cry of execration arose. The Company demanded justice. With English self-control it repressed irresponsible discussion by its members, and resolved, on June 16th, to trust to the state "to call for an account of the lives of the king's subjects." The governor refrained from speech until he was assured of the facts, and it was not until July 2d that he brought the matter officially before a general court of the Company.

The first feeling indeed was one of incredulity at so abominable an outrage on innocent men. King James "apprehended the fact to be so foul . . . he could not believe it," and, when convinced, threatened to extort reparation from Holland. At the Royal Council table "sundry of the greatest shed tears." But James had resolved to break with Spain, in wrath at the treatment of Prince Charles on his knight-errant quest at

Madrid for a Spanish wife in 1623. War with Spain meant an alliance with Holland, whose twelve years' truce with Spain had also expired. Dutch envoys were, indeed, at that moment in London, negotiating a treaty of offence and defence. So the king and his Council dried their eyes, and the Dutch diplomats joyfully returned home, praising the good-will of a monarch who had said not a word about "the late accident at Amboyna." Nor were courtiers wanting who blamed the Company for raising a difficulty "when his Majesty had resolved to aid the Dutch."

Very different was the temper of the nation. On July 2, 1624, the governor of the Company declared that assuredly "God the Avenger of all such bloody acts will in His due time bring the truth to light"—"the unspeakable tyrannies done upon those unfortunate men, which is able to amaze the Christian world." They still hoped that the king would help them; but their best comfort was that when man is at the weakest then God is strongest. On July 9th a general court of the Company decided that unless justice were "done on those Dutch that have in so great fury and tyranny tortured and slain the English," the Company must wind up and "fetch home what they have in the Indies." A petition in this sense was voted to the king —"and according to his answer and proceeding the trade to stop or proceed." On July 11th they waited on the king in his bedchamber with the memorial, together with "A True Relation," and received his promise of "a speedy reparation from the Dutch by the strength of his own arm, if they did it not suddenly themselves."

The cry for revenge had gathered a strength which not even James could resist. Chamberlain, the Horace Walpole of his time, wrote to the English ambassador

MARWARI MERCHANTS, OR TRADERS OF THE INDIES.

in Holland that "we should stay or arrest the first Indian ship that comes in our way, and hang up upon Dover cliffs" as many Dutchmen as had taken part in the outrage, "and then dispute the matter afterwards. For there is no other course to be held with such manner of men, as neither regard law nor justice, nor any other respect of equity or humanity, but only make gain their god." The Company was believed to have collapsed. No man would pay in any money to it. If the king would not help, it was wildly propounded at a general court on July 22d, to "join with the Portugals and root the bloody Dutch out of the Indies."

The "True Relation" presented to James on July 11, 1624, had touched the sentimental fibre in his weak nature. On July 16th he promised to make stay of Dutch vessels if satisfaction were not given, and even offered to become himself a shareholder in the Company, and to allow its ships to sail under the royal standard. This offer of greatness thrust upon it, the Company respectfully declined. The king meanwhile ordered his ambassador at The Hague to demand satisfaction from the States-General before August 12th, under threat of reprisals by hanging, or even "an irreconcilable war."

These were brave words, and if the Dutch Government had believed they would be followed by action, they might have proved decisive. For the outrage of Amboyna had come as an unpleasant surprise to the Dutch Company, and as a serious embarrassment to the Dutch Government. The governor-general at Batavia spoke his mind as freely as he dared to Van Speult. The Company in Holland, while making the best case they could against the English claims for compensation, refrained from sending back Coen to the East, although they had reappointed him governor-general in 1624. Members of the States-General openly expressed their disgust. The Prince of Orange wished that Van Speult with all his council had been hanged on a gibbet before they began "to spell this tragedy."

The States-General accordingly appointed deputies to treat with our ambassador. But an English observer wrote that, although the king spoke valiantly, he could wish his Majesty would say less, so that he would do more. The Dutch deputies played on his irresolution, and the time allowed for redress expired. When at length, on October 15th, a royal warrant was issued for the seizure of Flemish ships, our ambassador at The Hague advised that this extremity should be avoided, and the Dutch were somehow warned of the danger. In November, 1624, the London Company officially informed the lord admiral that Holland ships were in the Straits of Dover, but they were allowed to pass unharmed.

The English Company was forced to realize that, in trusting to the royal support, it leaned on a broken reed. In July it had demanded satisfaction under three heads: justice against the murderers, compensation for injuries, and absolute separation from the Dutch Company in the East. In October it despondently reduced its claims to the safe removal of the English from Batavia; the question of jurisdiction and Council of Defence; and the right to erect forts, and to be treated by the Dutch as allies and friends. James would not fight, and the Dutch knew it. They were willing enough to accept the first condition and allow the safe removal of the English from Batavia. But, while dangling before us a compromise, they would never surrender their sovereign jurisdiction in the Spice Islands or allow the English to erect fortifications. On March 25, 1625, King James died.

By this time the facts were well known in England. A certain simplicity in Towerson's character gave additional pathos to his death. He had sailed on the Com-

PALACE OF JAHANGIR AT AGRA.

pany's second voyage in 1604 and obtained his admission as a freeman *gratis* in recognition of long service. Eighteen checkered years brought him to the chief agency at Amboyna in 1622, with a salary of £10 a month. Once indeed he had emerged for a moment. Having married the Indian widow of Captain Hawkins, he attempted for a time to make a figure not justified either by her position or his own. In 1617 Sir Thomas

Roe, our ambassador to the Moghul Emperor Jahangir, wrote that Towerson "is here arrived with many servants, a trumpet, and more show than I use." In 1620 we find him back in England vainly soliciting the command of a ship, and returning to the Archipelago along with other factors in "the great cabin of the *Anne*."

The contemporary records show that he had not gained caution with years. Arriving at Amboyna in May, 1622, he became a close friend of the Dutch Governor Van Speult and gave him his entire confidence. In June of that year, as we saw, Van Speult was on the lookout for conspiracies and asking the Dutch governor-general at Batavia for leave to deal with them "suitably, unhesitatingly, and immediately." In September Towerson, on the other hand, wrote to the English president at Batavia in warm terms of Van Speult's "courtesies" and "love." He asks our president to send Van Speult a complimentary letter, together "with some beer or a case of strong waters, which will be very acceptable to him."

The president and council at Batavia saw more of the game. "In such kind of courtesy," they replied in December, 1622, "we know he is free enough, but in your main affairs you will find him a subtle man." There was to be no beer or case of strong waters for Van Speult. On the contrary, "be careful you be not circumvented in matters of importance, through his dissembling friendship." This warning they followed up next month by commanding Towerson and his subordinates to quit Amboyna. "Prepare and make yourself ready to come away from thence with all the rest of the factors in the Dutch ship, except two you may leave there at Amboyna to keep house until our further order."

Meanwhile Towerson continued his unsuspecting course. On January 1, 1623, he gave his official dinner to the little English group at Amboyna—the regular New Year's Day party which was to serve the Dutch fiscal as a ground-work for the alleged conspiracy. How far any thoughts of seizing Amboyna were from the minds of the English may be known by the letter of our president and council in March, 1622, to the Company, desiring to retire even from Batavia; by Brockedon's petition in August, 1622, for leave to return home, as he could "live no longer under the insolence of the Dutch;" and by the orders of January, 1623, to Towerson and other outlying agencies to withdraw to Batavia with the English under their charge. Towerson, "a sincere, honest, and plain man without malice," as one of the Amboyna free burghers and a servant of the Dutch Company described him, discerned not the signs of the times, and the letter ordering him to leave Amboyna was intercepted by the Dutch governor Van Speult. So he went to his death—"that honest good man, Captain Towerson, whom I think in my conscience was so upright and honest toward all men, that he has harboured no ill will of any."

Such a character is pretty sure of sympathy from the English middle classes, always indulgent to sturdy mediocrity, especially of the jovial sort. The story

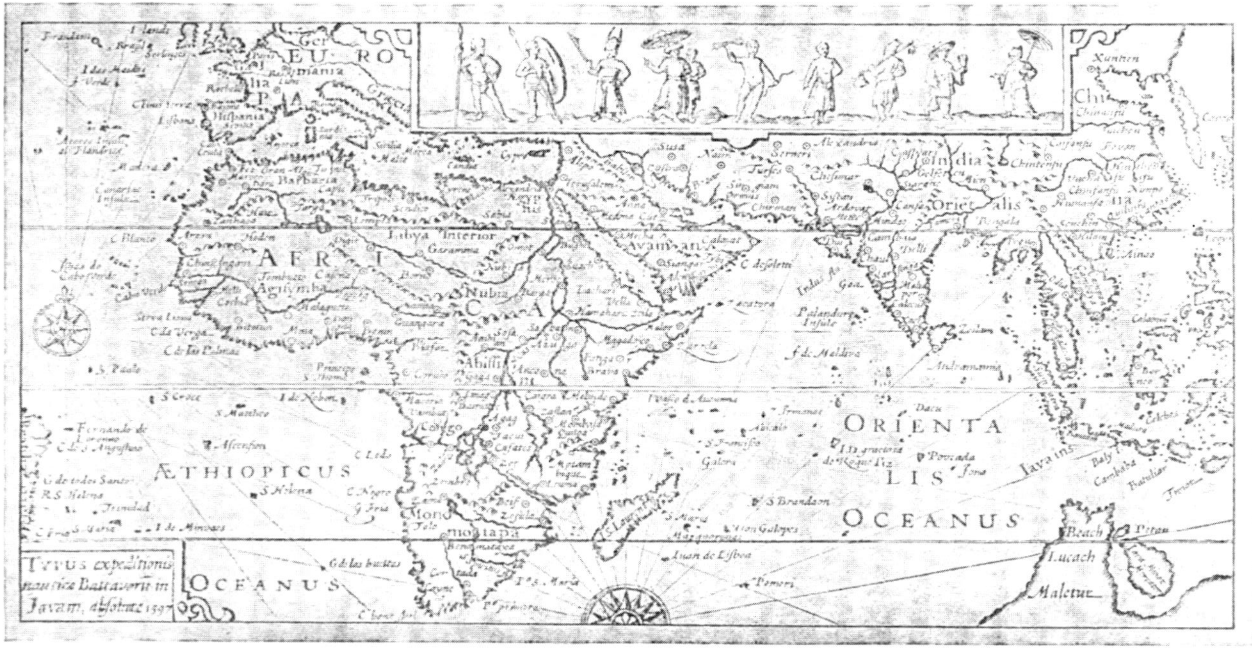

DE HOUTMAN'S MAP OF THE SEA ROUTE TO INDIA, BATAVIA, AND JAVA, IN 1597.

of Amboyna gathered round his name, until it reached Dryden's version of a murderous plot by Van Speult against Towerson in revenge for his killing Van Speult's son in a duel. In 1625 the legend was still a long way from this climax. But the last weeks of King James's life had been harassed by popular demonstrations. In February, 1625, the Dutch living in London complained to the lords of the Council that on the coming Shrove Tuesday they would be in danger from the fury of the people. Besides the pamphlets spread broadcast, a play was to be publicly acted setting forth the sufferings of the English; and a great picture had been painted, "lively, largely, and artificially," of their tortures and execution. The reins were falling from the old king's hands, and the Council gently admonished the Company not to exhibit this picture—at least till Shrove Tuesday be passed.

Next month, March, 1625, Charles succeeded to the throne. The main business of our ambassador at The Hague, Sir Dudley Carleton (afterwards Viscount Dorchester), was to strengthen the alliance of Holland with England against Spain, and he groaned audibly over the new labours and awkward questions to which the Amboyna imbroglio gave rise. Charles, keenly resentful of his personal treatment when in quest of a wife at Madrid, was eager to send a fleet to the Spanish coast, and promised large subsidies to the Protestant league in the North. The Amboyna difficulty had to be got out of the way, and in September, 1625, Charles agreed to make no reprisals on the Dutch ships for eighteen months, and at the same time appeased the London Company by promising that if, by that time, justice were not done, he would proceed to hostilities. This is shown by the treaty of Southampton, September 7, 1625.

But before the expiration of the eighteen months Charles had quarrelled with his Parliament and found a war with France on his hands. The Dutch were masters of the situation and they knew it. So far from

A TYPICAL EASTERN SCENE.

their giving satisfaction for Amboyna, Coen went out as governor-general for a second time in March, 1627, in spite of the protests of the English Company, who regarded his policy as the main source of their sorrows. When in April, 1627, the States-General were reminded that the eighteen months had elapsed, they dexterously got the question transferred to the law courts, and offered to proceed by way of a legal prosecution against the Amboyna judges who had sentenced the English to death.

Here they were on safe ground. Preliminary difficulties at once arose. The Dutch naturally insisted that the tribunal should be a Dutch one sitting in Holland. King Charles objected to his subjects being required to leave their country and prosecute before a foreign court beyond the seas. The feeling both in England and Holland was that, while the States-General would gladly have seen the matter settled, the directors of the Dutch Company were so intermingled with the Dutch Government that no justice would be done.

English protests against the re-appointment of Coen passed unheeded, and in August, 1627, Carleton despaired of redress from a government controlled by the votes of the interested parties, among whom "one oar which holds back, stops more than ten can row forward." In September, however, a tribunal of seven Dutch judges was constituted, three from the high and four from the provincial council.

Meanwhile Charles, with the rising tide in Parliament and in the nation against him, was anxious to keep the London Company his friends. In a moment of vigour, he stayed three Dutch ships off Cowes (September, 1627) and held them fast for eleven months, although threatened with a Dutch fleet to bring them away. The English Company declared that, if his Majesty let the Dutch ships go, it were better for the Company to abandon the trade. But the fit of royal resolution passed, and the king, in sore straits for money, suddenly released the Dutch ships in August, 1628: it was rumoured, for a gratification of £30,000. In vain his Majesty tried to soften the blow by the unprecedented compliment of sending the lords of the Council to a court meeting of the Company to explain that the release was due to an "extraordinary matter of State." The directors of the Dutch Company gave out as far back as March, 1628, that they had arranged for the release of the ships on the condition of their redeeming his Majesty's jewels.

The Company now knew that, if they had little to expect from the Dutch tribunal, they had nothing to hope from the king. The Dutch also knew it. In November, 1628, his Majesty feebly suggested, in reply to the repeated demands of the Dutch for the English witnesses to go over to Holland, that the Dutch judges should come to England under a safe-conduct—a proposal which merely furnished a good ground for further delay.

A year later, having sunk into still deeper difficulties with the Parliament and the nation, Charles yielded to the demands of the foreigner and sent over the witnesses. But he tried to save his royal honour by explaining that he had never submitted to the jurisdiction of the Dutch judges, although he would prefer to receive reparation at their hands than by any other means. The English ambassador must be present in the Dutch court; the English witnesses must not be questioned on other articles than those on which they had already been examined in his Majesty's Court of Admiralty; the Dutch judges, when ready to deliver sentence,. must inform the king of it, so that he might weigh and consider its import. The Dutch tribunal naturally refused to concede these points. The king had put not only himself but also the English nation in the wrong by his method of procedure, and again the Dutch knew it.

His Majesty struggled for a time in the meshes he had woven around himself. In December, 1629, he insisted on reserving the final sentence either to himself or to a joint bench of English and Dutch judges, on the strength of the treaty of 1619. The Dutch quite truly rejoined that the treaty contained not a single article which implied joint jurisdiction in criminal cases, but only in what concerned the joint defence and trade. While the preliminaries were thus spun out from 1627 to 1630, the six Amboyna councillors who were supposed to be on their trial figured as patriots to their nation. The English witnesses, still unheard, were sunk in debt to obtain food from day to day. They mournfully complained to the Privy Council that they had attended in Holland for twelve months, that they were now destitute and like to be cast into prison, while their wives and children were perishing miserably. In March, 1631, the British ambassador at The Hague reported that in the Amboyna business all was silence.

It is doubtful, even if the Amboyna council had been promptly and impartially tried, whether the London Company would have obtained substantial redress. It is certain that no court administering the law then in force in Europe could have condemned the judges to death for the Amboyna executions. The two grounds which underlay the English contention were badly chosen. As a matter of fact, the Amboyna council had exercised a lawful jurisdiction, and torture was not only allowed, but enjoined by the law which they were bound to administer. The Dutch Company's charter

CAPE TOWN AND HARBOUR.
(Copyright by Underwood and Underwood, New York.)

of 1602 empowered it to appoint public prosecutors in the name of the States-General for the conduct of judicial business in its fortresses beyond the Cape of Good Hope. The ordinances for the Dutch governor-general in 1617 authorized him not only to execute all civil and criminal sentences, but also to delegate this function to the subordinate councils and proper officers of settlements at which the governor-general and council could not be present. In 1619 instructions had been duly given to Van Speult to administer justice as governor of Amboyna in civil and criminal cases. They were further enforced by the Dutch governor-general's express sanction to Van Speult in October, 1622, to deal unhesitatingly with conspiracies.

A candid examination of the Anglo-Dutch treaty of 1619 shows that its jurisdiction clause referred only to questions of trade and joint defence, and left the criminal and civil jurisdiction untouched. Nor could the pronouncement of King James in 1623 seriously affect the issue, for the Dutch repudiated it as never having been accepted by (perhaps not even communicated to) their representatives. The States-General consistently maintained their civil and criminal jurisdiction in their settlements throughout the Spice Archipelago. As a matter of fact, the English in the Dutch settlements had been steadily subjected to that jurisdiction, although they groaned under it, and their very complaints to the directors in London prove their practical submission to its most irksome forms.

The general law of Europe at that time prescribed judicial torture as a proper and an almost necessary means for arriving at the truth. Dutch jurisprudence went so far as to declare that, in cases similar to that of Amboyna, a public prosecutor could demand sentence of death only on the confession of the accused.

The judges therefore, after satisfying themselves by independent proof of the guilt of the accused, had to obtain his confession; without torture if possible, by torture if not. But the Dutch ordinances of 1570 provided safeguards against the abuse of this method, and insisted on *indicia sufficientia ad torturam*, or a reasonable presumption of guilt before the torture was resorted to.

In England torture, although unrecognized by the common law, was employed in state trials by the Privy Council or High Commission Court in virtue of the royal prerogative. "The rack seldom stood idle in the Tower," writes Hallam, "for all the latter part of Elizabeth's reign." Lord Burleigh defended its use, as the accused "was never so racked but that he was perfectly able to walk and to write;" and "the warders, whose office and act it is to handle the rack, were ever by those that attended the examinations specially charged to use it in so charitable a manner as such a thing might be." "In the highest cases of treason," wrote Lord Bacon in 1603, "torture is used for discovery and not for evidence."

James I had perhaps less right than any other English sovereign to complain of its use by the Dutch. As King of Scotland he had not only sanctioned torture in alleged cases of conspiracy and witchcraft, but had in 1596 authorized even a subordinate court—the provost and baillies of Edinburgh—to try rioters by torture. As King of England he had in 1605 racked Guy Fawkes, *per gradus ad ima*, and in 1615 the aged Puritan Peacham had been examined " in torture, between tortures, and after torture." In the same year O'Kennan was put to the rack in Dublin by commission of the king's deputy. In each one of his three kingdoms James had used torture, and he defended it with his " own princely pen."

Even such details as the Dutch complaint that John Clarke must be " a devil " or " a witch," because he stubbornly refused to confess under torment, are reproduced in the English trials. On January 21, 1615, Lord Bacon condoled with his Majesty on the obstinacy of the mangled Peacham, " whose raging devil seems to be turned into a dumb devil." Lord Burleigh's defence of the rack on the ground that it was mercifully administered and that the sufferer was always " able to walk and to write " afterwards, is an exact anticipation of the Amboyna judge's plea of the " civil " character of the water-torture.

Yet if history must allow that the Dutch had jurisdiction, and that under that jurisdiction the use of torture was lawful, it must also declare that a grievous miscarriage of justice had taken place. It is admitted that the record discloses grave irregularities in procedure—irregularities so serious that if an appeal had been allowed they might have sufficed to quash the trial. How far they were due to the careless character of the record itself will ever remain undecided. There was certainly an absence of the *indicia sufficientia ad torturam*, or reasonable presumption of guilt, which would have justified torture under the Dutch law. The confession of the Japanese soldier which formed the ground of the whole proceeding was signed on the day of his torture in defiance of the Dutch ordinances of July 15, 1570, and it was attested by all the judges, although one of them (Wyncoop) was admittedly not in Amboyna on that day. The minutes make no mention of the witnesses being confronted with each other after torture, and of their reaffirming their confessions made under torture, as required by the Dutch law.

Above all, if the English statements on oath are accepted, the whole evidence from first to last was wrung forth by torture or fear of torture. If the Dutch counter-statements be preferred, the great mass of evidence was thus obtained. Of the two witnesses not subjected to torture, according to the Dutch account, one, Edward Collins, swore that he had been tortured, and produced testimony on oath to his dismal outcries. The other, the invalid Beaumont, declared that he had confessed only after he had been tied up for torture, and that he repeated his confession at Batavia to save his own life after the death of the victims had placed them beyond reach of further harm. The survivors consistently affirmed that the only evidence against them at their trial was derived from confessions under torture; confessions which, according to the English depositions on oath, were withdrawn after the torture; and which were solemnly affirmed to be false in the dying declarations of the sufferers.

It is not needful to assume that the Amboyna Council wickedly, and against their conscience, condemned the victims to death. Van Speult, as we have seen, was on the lookout for conspiracies, when he and his fellow councillors were suddenly transferred into the judges of men who had been their keen trade-rivals and the great obstacle to the Dutch supremacy in the

THE DURBAR OF AN INDIAN RULER.

Archipelago. Among Eastern races the king or governor was both ruler and judge, and the early European settlements in Asia found themselves compelled firmly to unite all functions, executive and judicial, in the hands of one man or body of men. Cases inevitably occurred in which they were practically judges in their own cause; apt in moments of public danger or fear to bring their passions and preconceptions as governors to their seats on the bench. The Amboyna trial was such a case. It stands on the forefront of our history in the East as an example of the danger of combining the executive and the judicial authority in the same hands. That danger the English have striven to guard against by the separation of judicial and executive offices—a process commenced almost from the foundation of their territorial rule in India, yet reaching its final stages only in our own time.

But if we view with charity the cruel blunder of the Amboyna Council as a whole, it is difficult to extend to either the governor or the prosecuting fiscal the benefit of the doubt. The fiscal, Isaac de Bruyne, appears throughout the records in a sinister light. Intent on obtaining a conviction, he constantly urged on Van Speult, and forced incriminating answers upon the witnesses till the council itself had to interpose. His record of the trial was so irregular and incomplete as to render impossible a fair judicial review of the proceedings. On the face of the record as it stands, the accused were improperly condemned. Bruyne's conduct called forth the reprobation of his superiors at Amboyna, and in the English depositions he appears as "the greatest adversary against the English." Whatever may have been Van Speult's own preconception as to their guilt during the first excited days of the prosecution, he can scarcely, after the seizure of the English factory and the perusal of Towerson's correspondence with the English president at Batavia, have believed in the plot. But by that time he may have felt that he had gone too far to retrace his steps. Or he may have simply been one of those commonplace officials who jump to conclusions and then remain obdurate to facts. His interception of the letter from our president at Batavia ordering the withdrawal of the English from Amboyna, was only the last act in the suppression of proof of innocence.

The Dutch authorities themselves felt uneasy lest Van Speult should be examined as to his share in the business. On the expiration of his term of office at Amboyna, he had hardly returned to Batavia when a rumour arrived of a ship in the Straits of Sunda bearing a joint commission from the king and States-General for the despatch of Van Speult to Europe. He was hastily sent off to the western coast of India, whence he proceeded with an expedition to the Red Sea, and he died at Mocha, carrying his secret to the grave.

Meanwhile the English, with their agents drawn in from the Spice Archipelago, and huddled together at Batavia, waited wistfully for redress from home. They waited in vain. News of the Amboyna tragedy reached Batavia on June 20, 1623. At length, having suffered nineteen more months of insults and exactions, their ships dogged by Dutch vessels at sea and cut off from trade on shore, they resolved to quit "this perfidious people," and, cost what it might, to seek shelter elsewhere. Some of them found refuge on the Indian coast, and in October, 1624, the miserable remnant sailed to the unhealthy Lagundy islets on the southeast of Sumatra.

There, amid terrible privations, yet stubbornly "affiant of a happy plantation," they renamed the little group Charles's Islands, and held out against fever and dysentery for eight months, dying "like sheep infected" under the equatorial sun and rain. In May, 1625, the skeleton survivors were so reduced as to implore the clemency of the Dutch, who in pity fetched them back to Batavia. The commander Verholt, be it recorded, showed them all "care and courtesy," although he himself and many of his crew caught the disease. Nor did Dutch compassion end with their bare deliverance. They received the rescued men with kindness and granted them a factory house at a moderate price, the Dutch governor-general and our president, in an effusion of good feeling, exchanging chains of gold.

The Dutch had, in fact, accomplished the two fixed purposes of their policy—our expulsion from the Spice Archipelago and our complete subjection at their Batavian headquarters in Java. Their harshness had been deliberately designed to this end, and, with the exception of Van Speult's judicial slaughter at Amboyna, they had kept fairly within their treaty rights. Their double object being now achieved, they allowed their national good nature free scope. But the excess of cordiality wore off, and the English soon became impatient of the restraints which the Dutch thought themselves entitled to impose. In July, 1627, we find our President Hawley bitterly complaining of the treatment meted out to his countrymen.

Their position was indeed an impossible one, and the Company at home, sick of King Charles's fair words, realized this fact. In November, 1626, it proposed to abolish its factory at Batavia and to establish one under the protection of the King of Bantam. In

JAVANESE PRINCES.

January, 1628, these orders reached Batavia, and the English, putting the relics of their property on board ship, sailed to Bantam, where they were welcomed by the native prince. The sad fortunes of our Bantam factory, its repeated reduction by the London Company to a subordinate post, its blockades by the Dutch, and the gradual but sure withdrawal of its trade to our settlements on the Indian coast, belong to a later period. Its history may, however, be summed up in a single sentence. As the executions at Amboyna proclaimed the triumph of the Dutch in the Spice Islands, so the fate of Bantam declared the supremacy of the Dutch in the sea-approaches to the Far East.

By 1631 all hope of judicial redress for the torture and execution of our countrymen at Amboyna had flickered out. In 1633, and again in 1638, Charles, urged by the despairing Company, reverted to feeble attempts at negotiation, with equal unsuccess.[1] Innocent Englishmen had been tortured and executed under the forms of a foreign law, and for their slaughter redress could not be obtained either by diplomacy or by judicial proceedings. From the first, the Dutch were resolved not to yield, save to force of arms. As they had speedily discovered that James I would not fight, so they gradually found out that Charles I could not fight.

[1] An English writer, who is not a lawyer and who has spent most of his life in the practical duties of Indian administration, should speak with diffidence as to the forms of Dutch procedure in the early seventeenth century. I have, therefore, taken the precaution to consult a Dutch jurist, Dr. Bisschop, who combines accurate historical research with a judicial training. He states, and quotes Dutch legal authorities for his opinion, that in extraordinary proceedings, in which the accused were examined without witnesses first being heard, the confessions of the accused were necessary for conviction, and that torture could be legitimately resorted to in order to obtain such confessions. The Amboyna trial came practically under this category, and the evidence from first to last was obtained by torture. But the Dutch law recognized the danger of a miscarriage of justice arising out of confessions thus wrung forth, and it provided safeguards accordingly. These safeguards were explicit in form and essential to the validity of the proceedings. They were disregarded in the Amboyna trial, although the prosecuting fiscal, in the words of the Dutch Governor-General and Council, "calls himself a lawyer, and was taken into the Company's service as such."

It was not till the unhappy distractions of the second Stuart's reign came to their tragic close, and until the Dutch found that a real man again ruled England, that they conceded to Cromwell, after war, what a little firmness might have secured at the outset to James.

At length, in April, 1654, the States-General agreed "that justice be done upon those who were partakers or accomplices in the massacre of the English at Amboyna, as the Republic of England is pleased to term that fact, provided any of them be living." Cromwell brooked no delay. Within five months all claims and counter-claims arising during forty-one years had been examined. In August the general damages of £85,000 were awarded to the London Company, together with £3615 to the heirs of the men done to death at Amboyna; and Pularoon was restored to English rule.

But this tardy justice failed to efface Amboyna from the English mind. The spectres of the tortured victims stood between the two great Protestant powers during a century. The memory of a great wrong unredressed and of innocent blood unavenged embittered their trade rivalry, intensified each crisis of political strain, and furnished a popular cry for two wars. Dryden's "Tragedy of Amboyna," produced in the fiftieth year after the execution, has been not unfairly described as his one literary effort which is wholly worthless except as a curiosity. Yet it serves to show how the story deepened into a darker hue with age.

The opening dialogue between Van Speult and the Dutch fiscal reveals their hatred to the English. Van

Speult's son, whom Towerson has rescued at sea, plots with the fiscal against the life of his preserver, and, after again being saved from death by Towerson, ravishes the Englishman's bride and is thereupon killed by him in a duel. Van Speult, in revenge, invents the story of the plot. The victims are tortured on the stage, fiercely reviled by the governor, and led off to execution. On his way to death Towerson breaks forth in a prophetic strain, foretelling the vengeance of his countrymen and the ruin and downfall of the Dutch. The characters are coarsely drawn from the "True Relation;" the picture presented of the Dutch is grossly unfair. But it struck a chord of popular feeling, and responded to an antipathy which had hardened and set into a national tradition.

That tradition not only affected our internal and dynastic politics, but it profoundly influenced the march of events in Europe. If Holland and England had been friends at heart instead of occasional allies by interest, the aggressions of Louis XIV would have encountered a very different strength of resistance. Our Charles II would scarcely have dared to remain the dependent of France. James II would perhaps have shrunk from forcing a Catholic reaction on England. The memory of Amboyna wrought like a fever on the trade-rivalry of the two Protestant sea powers. The friendship of France might mean court corruption and Popery, but between England and Holland, as long as that bloody memory lived, there could be no real friendship at all. Politicians and poets appealed to the middle-class hatred of the Dutch as against the middle-class hatred of Rome. Amboyna is thus disclosed as one of the influences which lured on the Stuarts to the Revolution, and as one of the remote secret springs of the age of Louis XIV.

Nor had Amboyna less important consequences for the Dutch. The overthrow of the English in the Spice Archipelago and their subjection in Java enabled the Holland Company to create a colonial system which, for frank indifference to human suffering, stands out in the history of European settlements across the seas. The fault was not the fault of the Dutch nation, but of the particular period when the chance of a great colonial empire came to it. The Catholic tradition of conversion by conquest, cruel as were its practices, had given place to the industrial idea of conquest for trade.

Neither Spain nor Portugal, with their record of blood in the Eastern and the Western worlds, nor England, with its subsequent slave traffic, can afford to cast stones. But the comparative isolation of Holland in the East, and the absence of any strong native power in the Archipelago like that of the Moghul dynasty in India, enabled the Dutch to work out the industrial idea of conquest to its logical results. The same isolation enabled them to perpetuate that idea, after it had been profoundly modified by a humanitarian awakening in Europe. It survived as a relic of a century when the Protestant nations of the Continent, wearied with religious strife, lost sight for a time of that spiritual brotherhood of man which shot rays across the darkness of Portuguese misrule, and which had burned up afresh before the foundation of British territorial sway in India. Jan Pieterszoon Coen, the chief founder of the Dutch colonial system, became governor-general in

TOMB OF THE MOGHUL OFFICIAL ITMAD-AD-DAULAH, AT AGRA.

1618—the date taken by European history for the commencement of the Thirty Years' War.

Coen has left in his own words a detailed description of the fabric which he designed. The Dutch charter expired in January, 1623, and on the 21st of that month the great governor-general, as the last act of his first term of office, drew up his political testament for the benefit of his countrymen in the form of instructions left with Peter de Carpentier, governor-general, and the Council of the Indies, and dated Batavia,

21 - 31, January, 1623. He realized that the sea-power of Holland in the Archipelago must rest on a territorial basis with a territorial revenue, the absence of which had drawn forth from Cosme Annes, nearly a hundred years earlier (1549), the Portuguese lament: "We sit still, perishing without lands out of which to support ourselves or find shelter." Albuquerque discerned the same need a century before. But Coen deliberately worked out what Albuquerque had perceived, and, unlike Albuquerque, he was backed by a nation which loyally supported its great servants in the East.

He cherished no illusions as to how such a territorial sea-empire was to be acquired and maintained. It was easy to bring the scattered islands under subjection. The problem was to people them with workers. The idea of settling Dutchmen and Dutchwomen in sufficient numbers, although it had its attractions for Coen as for the other colonizing spirits of that age, he saw to be impracticable. He anticipated the conclusion which some of the European nations are only now reaching after long and cruel experience, that agricultural emigrants from the temperate zone perish in the tropics. The lands of the equator can be tilled only by equatorial races. The heathen whom the Papal Bulls had given to the Portuguese for an inheritance, to be converted with a rod of iron or dashed to pieces like a potter's vessel, were to Coen merely a cheap labour-force. The "ingathering of a multitude of people from all parts to people our country withall" was his first object, and of far more consequence, he declared, than the buying of cloths and goods.

This object he proposed to accomplish by three distinct methods: the enslavement of conquered islands, the purchase of slaves from the African and Asiatic continents, and the seizure of slaves on their coasts. The first method needs but the single comment, that it went much further than the subjection of the native races enforced by the Portuguese. As regards the second, orders for the buying of slaves had been given in 1614; Coen resolved to carry them out on a large scale. "Divers fleets" were now to be sent to the Coromandel coast, to Madagascar, and to the African seaboard, to purchase as many slaves, especially young people, as could be got. This buying of slaves was to go forward before any other work, to the extent of "many thousands, yea, to an infinite number."

The third method, by seizure, was to be conducted by a squadron on the Chinese coast. The shore-dwellers, especially the women and children, were to be carried away for the peopling of Batavia, Amboyna, and Banda. "Herein will be a great service done for the Company, and by this means will be found all the charge of the war." The Chinese slaves might be redeemed for sixty reals (£13 10*s.*) apiece. "But by no means you must not suffer any women to return to China, or any other part out of the Company's jurisdiction, but with them to people the same." As the Dutch supremacy firmly established itself, a fourth system of recruitment was added, by treaty provisions for a tribute in full-grown slaves.

The Dutch industrial system in the East, thus

A TROPICAL SCENE IN INDIA.

founded on the most rigorous forms of slavery, was eventually softened through successive stages of forced labour. It produced for a time enormous profits. A tropical soil was made to yield as it had never yielded before, and its fruits were monopolized by Holland.

As respects European rivals, the restrictions which the Anglo-Dutch still imposed on Coen, in January, 1623, were removed by the tragedy of Amboyna in the next month, and by the withdrawal of the English factories from the Spice Archipelago. As regards native competition, the islanders were compelled to root up their clove and nutmeg trees, where they seemed to threaten the profits of the Dutch. The produce of the most fertile regions in the world, cultivated on the severest system of human toil, was secured to the Dutch and to the Dutch alone.

While Coen founded the colonial empire of Holland on the sure basis of the soil, he strengthened it by all the devices of a skilful administration—by a lucrative coasting trade with the African and Asiatic continents, by a great sea commerce with Europe, and by a well-planned system of tolls and local taxation. The rich island empire which he thus projected, he secured by fortresses, built and maintained by the cheap labour of prisoners and slaves. Coen stands out from among all men of European race in the Asia of his day—a statesman of the clearest vision, and an administrator of the firmest hand, half-way between the Portuguese Albuquerque in the sixteenth century and the French Dupleix or the English Warren Hastings, in the eighteenth. But he could not rise above the morals of his time, and his strong personality during a double tenure of office impressed the stamp of a cruel age on the colonial system of his country. His crime, or his misfortune, was that he stereotyped in Dutch India the disregard for human suffering which brutalized Europe during the Thirty Years' War.

Holland was the first European country to send a steady supply of really able men to the East, and she supported them by force of arms. James I would not and Charles I could not fight. The English East India Company was still a body of private adventurers for whose benefit Parliament felt by no means eager to go to war. In spite of the long list of lords and gentlemen who swelled the subscription book of the Company, in spite of the outburst of wrath and indignation which the news of Amboyna aroused in London, England had not yet learned to look upon her Indian trade as a national concern. Holland had, and she was willing to make sacrifices and to screen crimes, in order to maintain her position in Asia.

ARMS OF THE EAST INDIA COMPANY.

CHAPTER V

THE COMPANY AND THE KING

1623 - 1649 A. D.

IN 1628, while the Petition of Right was giving shape to the conflict between the king and the Commons, the fortunes of the Company reached a low ebb. During the preceding five years one blow after another had fallen upon it, at home and abroad. In the Far East its servants saved their lives only by abandoning their settlements in Japan. In the Spice Archipelago we have seen them tortured and slain at Amboyna, and driven forth from the Clove Isles. In the Javanese Straits they had been decimated by disease at their ocean-refuge of Lagundy, and were brought back by the clemency of the Dutch to Batavia, only to quit it again after a further struggle with misery. On the Bay of Bengal, the native governor was inflicting on them the " foul injuries " which were to force them out of Masulipatam. On the opposite, or western, coast of India, their warehouses were ransacked and their chiefs at Surat imprisoned in irons; "to be," in the words of their president, "the shameful subjects of daily threats, revilings, scorns, and disdainful derisions."

At home, the finances of the Company threatened a collapse. Notwithstanding the profits of individual voyages, the value of its capital had in 1626 fallen over twenty per cent., and £100 of stock were not worth £80. Its shipping had decreased by one-third. The affrighted adventurers, seeing no end to their losses, would contribute but £40,000 instead of £200,000, or one-fifth of what they had formerly provided for the annual voyage, and in 1628 the Company could not obtain a subscription for a new joint-stock. It had already borrowed so heavily that no one would lend it more money on its common seal, and its managers had to carry on business by pledging their private credit. Internal dissensions rose high, and in 1627 the Company was constrained to "battulate" a brawling member (Mr. Thomas Smethwike), that is, to forbid him any more to come to its meetings or to trouble its house and courts. In June, 1628, the Company's debt amounted to £230,000, which was further increased to £300,000 by March, 1629, and the yearly interest to £20,000.

From outside it could hope for little support. To the country gentlemen the East India Company was a monopoly which drained England of its bullion in order to buy spices, luxuries, and toys. This "canker of the commonwealth," on which Malynes, in 1601, had laid a rough finger, with the threatening motto *sublata causa tollitur effectus*, became a stock theme for patriotic eloquence. According to another writer (the author of the "Trade's Increase," in 1615), the delusive reports of the India trade were but "the pleasing

INDIAN CARPENTERS AT WORK.

notes of the swans in Meander flood," which would in reality prove, like theirs, the dismal croaking of "greedy ravens and devouring crows." The Company, it was said, had cut down the oaks that should have built the royal ships; it had raised the price of timber for merchant vessels by five shillings a load; it was in truth "a parricide of woods." Its gains, "the price of blood," "bought with so many men's lives," had, the nation was assured, killed and worn out the mariners who formed the defence of England, and left a multitude of widows and orphans to an unhappy fate. "The whole land" was called to protest against the drain of bullion that "causeth the body of this commonwealth to be wounded sore." As the Portuguese "were the enemies of Christendom, for they carried the treasure of Europe to enrich the heathen," so the Company was the enemy of England, which, between the export of coin and the Dutch, had become a blind Belisarius begging by the wayside.

To these popular denunciations, many of them ill-founded, some of them insincere, the Company opposed an array of facts, convincing to the modern economist. But the English political economy of that day was a compound of mediæval tradition and national prejudice; the true principles of currency and commerce emerged only in the following century. Meanwhile the enemies of the India trade had mediæval tradition and national prejudice on their side. The fact that the Company's defence had to be conducted by its own servants or members deepened the popular distrust.

It was in vain that Sir Dudley Digges, in 1615, proved that the statements about the consumption of timber, the loss of mariners, and the export of coin were exaggerated, or compensated by counter benefits to the nation. For Sir Dudley Digges had been a candidate for the governorship of the Company in the preceding year. He did not help his case by insulting contrasts between "the idle drone and the greedy caterpillars" who lived at ease in England, and the "laborious bees" in the East who "bring the honey to the hive." Nor did the public take seriously his metaphor, which was destined to prove so true, of the Company as a "Hercules yet in the cradle." We must, indeed, distinguish between the young Sir Dudley Digges of 1615 dabbling in the City, and the mature Sir Dudley Digges who stood forth for the Commons in the impeachment of Buckingham, and gave voice to the nation on the Petition of Right. Yet Sir Dudley Digges of the East India Company, under the first Stuart king, came near to the principles by which Sir Dudley North of the Turkey Company, under the last Stuarts, anticipated the doctrines of Adam Smith. In the case alike of the earlier and the later Sir Dudley, the actual facts of our Eastern commerce supplied the basis for sounder economics.

Thomas Mun's "Discourse of Trade," in 1621, formed by far the ablest statement of the case on behalf of the adventurers. But to his contemporaries Mun appeared as a wealthy director of the Company, who was rewarded for his advocacy by the offer of the inspectorship of its factories in India. His arguments were in advance of the age, and as we shall find them reiterated in the Company's petition to Parliament in 1628, I need not pause over them here. On the public they had little effect. The Company still continued to be the Jason that had stolen away England's golden fleece of bullion. "The clamorous complaints," which induced Mun to come forward in its defence, continued as "loud as before," "the only remedy" being "to put down this trade."

Nor could the Company hope much from the king, to whose act of prerogative it owed its existence. The Crown had commenced anew the encroachments which James had on more than one occasion effusively relinquished. How far the royal aggression can be excused we shall presently examine. To the despondent adventurers it seemed to threaten the finishing stroke. It was bad enough that their interests should be the sport of an evasive foreign policy: thrown over in favour of Portugal when his Majesty sought a Spanish marriage; and sacrificed to a Dutch alliance when Prince Charles returned angry and sore from his wooing at Madrid. It also rankled that the Company should be bidden by a courtier, Sir William Heydon, and Endymion Porter, the groom of the prince's bedchamber, to carry to India two emissaries whom it believed to be rivals in trade. But when King James arrested its ships and stigmatized the directors as "pirates" because, under legal advice, they refused to comply with certain demands of the Crown, the situation grew well-nigh intolerable. The end came when Charles was found conniving at the opposition within the Company's own courts, and encouraging the "battulated" member, Smethwike, to raise the whole question of the Indian trade before his Majesty's Council. Meanwhile the Company, on the flood-tide of popular feeling which bore forward the Petition of Right, appealed in 1628 to Parliament.

Its "Remonstrance" begins almost in the language

of despair. It prays the House that "if the said trade be found unprofitable to the commonwealth it may be suppressed, and if otherwise that then it may be supported and continued by some public declaration." But it presently rises to a higher tone. Drawn up by Thomas Mun and revised by Sir John Coke, the memorial answers one by one all the objections that had been urged during the past twenty-eight years against the Company. It is in fact Mun's "Discourse of Trade," reduced to language of precision, and developing in detail economic arguments which Mun's book of 1621 had more timidly wrapped up.

A MOSLEM MERCHANT IN CEYLON.

So far from weakening the nation, the Company urged that its fleets formed a vast training school for the English marine, a magazine from which the royal navy could draw both men and munitions of war. That so far from decreasing the national wealth, it brought to England a store of Indian products of which only a portion was consumed at home, while the greater part was re-exported to other countries, at a large profit to the realm. Of £208,000 worth of pepper imported in 1627, no less than £180,000 worth was re-exported abroad. It urged that while the Crown thus secured an increase to its customs, the people were enabled to buy spices at much lower rates; although in some articles the Dutch interference had again doubled the prices. That the gentry gained by the increased exportation of wool and woolen stuffs, "which doth improve the landlords' rents." That the Company was in fact become a defence of the commonwealth, "to counterpoise the Hollanders' swelling greatness by trade, and to keep them from being absolute Lords of the Seas." It had also deprived Spain of the "incredible advantage of adding the traffique of the East Indies to the treasure of the West." That if the English trade with the Indies should fail, then other English commerce would fail with it, and pass into the hands of the Dutch.

The Company thus grounded its first appeal to Parliament on a broadly national basis. But the charge of draining the country of its bullion was more difficult to meet. In 1621, Mun had exposed the exaggerated character of this complaint, and shown that during the previous twenty years the Company shipped only half a million sterling, not in English coinage but in Spanish reals, while licensed to export three-quarters of a million. In 1628, in the Remonstrance to the Commons, he took a bolder stand. The Company declared that the export of bullion to buy Indian wares, which it resold to foreign nations at a great profit, was a good employment for the national treasure It declared that, since England had neither gold nor silver, she could acquire bullion only "by making our commodities which are exported, to overbalance in value the foreign wares which we consume." "It is not . . . the keeping of our money in the kingdom which makes a quick and ample trade, but the necessity and use of our wares in foreign countries, and our want of their commodities which causeth the vent and consumption on all sides."

"For," as Mun privately wrote, "if we only behold the actions of the husbandman in the seed-time when he casteth away much good corn into the ground, we will rather accompt him a madman than a husbandman; but when we consider his labours in the harvest, which is the end of his endeavours, we find the worth and plentiful encrease of his actions."

This early enunciation of the Mercantile System, which anticipated Colbert's acceptance of it by a quarter of a century, fell flat in 1628. Parliament was too busy with the Petition of Rights to spare time for the complaints of the Company. But even if it had had the leisure, it was too deeply ingrained with the old prejudice against exporting bullion, to be enticed by new-fangled economics. Four years previously, on a motion "to search the East India ships for money," the Company's friends were answered by tumultuous cries of "stay the money that they send out of the land," "search the books." Cheap pepper and cloves mattered little to the country gentlemen of England, battling for their liberties with the Crown.

To the people at large the Company represented the survival of a royal prerogative, which had grown unpopular even under Elizabeth, become intolerable under James, and was, in 1624, sternly curtailed by statute. A monopoly might be needful for the armed trade which was then the only trade possible in the East. Yet to the rising spirit of the nation, the exclusive privileges granted to the Company by King James seemed scarcely more bearable than those granted by the Borgian Pope to Portugal and Spain. Its sufferings, with the exception of the Amboyna outrage, touched no chord of popular sympathy. Up to 1628, books for or against the Company were published at intervals. But from its appeal to Parliament in 1628 onwards until 1640, I do not find that a single book or pamphlet in its interests issued from the press. Parliament and the nation left the Company severely alone to the king.

The aggressions of the early Stuarts on the Company, often denounced as mere acts of extortion, are disclosed by a dispassionate inquiry in a somewhat different light. The Crown regarded the Company as its own creation, and knew it to be in continual need of its support. It had made over to the Corporation a privilege of a highly marketable value—the monopoly of the Indian trade—which it could have sold and resold at large prices to successive groups of adventurers. The king also armed the Company with powers of military aggression on sea and land, and he had to maintain it by the royal power in what went near to a piratical warfare on the ships of friendly Christian nations.

The Crown expected in return, not only the stipulated customs which it would in any case have received from successive groups of adventurers, but also a complaisance to its creatures, and loans or gifts of money. This necessity for paying for what was in fact a curtailment of the trade-liberties of the nation continued long after the power of curtailment passed from the Crown to Parliament. Such payments grew, indeed, from rare and grudging benevolences to the first Stuart kings, into large and frequent loans to the constitutional government.

In dealing with the Company James I might scold, Charles I might sigh, and Charles II might laugh; but they all understood their power and were equally resolved to profit by it. "Did I deliver you from the complaint of the Spaniards and do you return me nothing?" James I replied angrily to the directors when they refused the two-tenths of the £100,000 worth of booty seized at Ormuz. The directors took legal advice, wriggled long on the hook, but in the end paid the £20,000 to his Majesty and the Lord High Admiral. James, indeed, was as ready to share the misfortunes of the Company as he was determined to profit by its successes. During the darkest days of Amboyna he offered to become a freeman of the Company, and to support it with the royal authority and the right of carrying the royal flag. The Company foresaw, however, that with so high a personage among them they would lose "the free election" of their own officers, who must in the end become the nominees of the king and court. They also feared being "drawn into actions of war" and costly enterprises of state. They thus avoided the rocks on which the French Companies afterwards suffered shipwreck, and humbly declined his Majesty's proposal.

The kingcraft which James I naïvely professed, Charles I feebly practised. His release, in 1628, of the Dutch ships which he had promised to hold fast as the sole means of securing redress for Amboyna, came like a stab in the dark to the Company. Nor did his unprecedented complaisance in sending the lords of his Council to Leadenhall Street to explain away the transaction avail more than to tinge resentment with contempt. The directors knew perfectly that it was the royal revenge for their Petition and Remonstrance to Parliament in the preceding spring. But Charles, unlike James, kept his temper and did not use bad words. Swallowing his wrath at the directors' appeal to Parliament, he assured them in July, 1628, that such was his love to commerce in general and to the Company in particular that he would not have them doubt of his protection, and meanwhile he would feel obliged for a loan of £10,000. As the loan was not forthcoming, he transferred his civilities to the Dutch. In the following month he was said to have taken their bribe of £30,000, and he certainly let their ships go.

Charles thus learned early in his reign that the Company, while ready to gratify the royal love of "varieties" by the gift of a leopard or other strange Indian

TRAVELLING SNAKE-CHARMERS AT SURAT.

beast, was not to be squeezed of hard cash. But his courtiers discovered more subtle means. The Company imported saltpetre, and this could not be sold till his

Majesty's pleasure was known as to whether he might want it for gunpowder, or until payments had passed secretly to the court. As the royal distresses increased he acted more vigorously, and in 1640, the Company having no money to lend him, he forced it to sell him on credit £65,000 worth of pepper, which he promptly resold for cash at a loss of £6000. His Majesty's profit on the transaction was nevertheless a handsome one, as all that the Company received from him seems to have been £13,000, certain disputed exemptions from customs dues, and the privilege of taking timber from the Forest of Dean.

So ingenious a device would not bear repetition. Charles, however, had already hit on a surer plan for making money out of the Indian trade. The charter of James I granted the monopoly to the Company for ever. But it contained a proviso for the resumption of the privilege, on three years' notice from the Crown, if the grant should not prove profitable to the realm. On this matter the king was the sole judge. He was surrounded by courtiers with their salaries in arrears, and by adventurers eager to show him a more excellent way, and to pay secret money for the permission to do so. How could he be sure that a Company, which constantly paraded its losses, was carrying on a trade profitable to the realm, unless he allowed others to try their hand? He had done many things for the Company, encouraged its efforts to raise fresh capital, issued royal proclamations to help it against its servants' private trade, written letters to Eastern potentates, negotiated with Spain and Holland on its behalf, offered to send an envoy to the Great Moghul, and was he to get nothing for his pains? By some such casuistry Charles seems to have felt justified in allowing his courtiers and their City friends to experiment in the Indian trade.

The records of the Company during his reign are full of the ignominious struggle which ensued. The king commenced cautiously by compelling the Company in 1630 to find a passage for the Earl of Denbigh, who had been seized by a desire to visit India and Persia; not altogether without an eye to business, as, on his return, he was reported to have landed sixty bales of indigo and other goods secretly at Dover, and conveyed them in carts to Southwark.

Four years after Denbigh's return, Prince Rupert, aged eighteen, appeared as the figurehead of a court clique for colonizing Madagascar, then regarded as a half-way house to India and within the limits of the Company's charter. This is proved by manuscript entries in the Court Book, under the date March 20, 1637. The Company's protests might have availed little; but the young adventurer's mother, the Queen of Bohemia, laughed at the scheme as a Quixote's isle of Barataria, "neither feasible, safe, nor honourable." So, in spite of a servile poem by Davenant, Prince Rupert, or "Prince Robert" as he appears in the Company's records, went off to the siege of Breda instead. Lord Arundell, who succeeded to the leadership of the project, not only proposed to plant a colony in Madagascar, but asked for a contract "to transport the Company's pepper and other commodities from thence to England." The Company politely thanked his lordship, said that it had enough ships of its own, and firmly refused a passage for him or his friends.

But it was not with noble and princely personages that the Company had mainly to strive. Wealthy merchants were now willing to stake their fortunes on breaking down the Company's monopoly, and they found gentlemen about the king's person ready, for a consideration, to gain his Majesty's ear. The most famous of these cabals of the City and Whitehall was Courten's Association; it had lasting consequences on the India trade, and it illustrates the hostile combinations to which the Company, as long as it depended on the royal favour, was exposed. The chief actors in the drama were Sir William Courten and Sir Paul Pindar, two London merchants, who between them "lent" the king £200,000; and with them was Endymion Porter, groom of the bedchamber and his Majesty's factotum for secret affairs.

William Courten started as a plain London trader, the son of a Flemish Protestant clothier who had found refuge in England under Elizabeth and prospered beneath her protecting rule. William learned business at Haarlem, and began usefully by marrying the deaf and dumb daughter of a Dutch merchant who brought him £60,000. Returning to London, he grew into a great merchant with ships trading to Portugal, the African coast, and the West Indies. He had the distinction in

1619 of being fined £20,000 by the Star Chamber for exporting gold—an experience sweetened after three years by a knighthood from James. This mingled taste of royal discipline and kingly favour led him to seek closer relations with the court, and in 1625 he modestly applied for a grant of the "Terra Australis Incognita," or Unknown South of the World. Three years later, letters patent, more limited in scope and discreetly addressed to the Earl of Pembroke—the late king's gentleman of the bedchamber, and a spirited company-promoter for Virginia, the Northwest Passage, South America, and elsewhere—were granted "in trust for Sir Wiliam Courten." The project failed, and Sir William, with a purse ever open to his Majesty's needs, obtained in 1635 a more promising license for the East Indian trade.

His principal partner in the adventure was Sir Paul Pindar, a man of good family, born after Elizabeth's accession and educated for the University, but with a natural genius for commerce. He learned the secrets of the Eastern trade during fifteen years of profitable businss in Venice and Italy, and practised them for nine years more as James's envoy, and the nominee of the Levant Company, in Turkey. He brought home so great a fortune that Buckingham fitted out Prince Charles for his wooing trip to Madrid with Pindar's diamonds, saying he would talk about payment afterwards. One fine jewel, valued at £35,000, Pindar was wont to lend James I to wear on state occasions; and in two transactions alone he handed over diamonds to the value of £26,000 on the payment-deferred system to Charles. His loans to his Majesty were reckoned at £100,000, besides moneys to the queen and royal

AN INDIAN TINSEL-WORKER.

children; for (as Carew wrote) "this Sir Paul never fails the king when he has most need." To so generous a financier a Stuart king could not stint his favours by scruples as to chartered rights.

The two merchants took into partnership an ally more influential than either. Endymion Porter, poetaster, courtier, speculator, virtuoso, patron of the Muses and of the Olympic Games on the Cotswold Hills, was a sort of Jacobean echo of Elizabethan Philip Sidney, with Zutphen left out. We have seen Sidney himself a defaulting subscriber to Northwestern Passages. Porter married the niece of Buckingham, accompanied the favourite and Prince Charles to Spain, and on Charles's succession to the crown became groom of the king's bedchamber. His portrait in the National Portrait Gallery shows a tall and graceful dilettante, with a face full of interest and intrigue, while another portrait of him in the same gallery displays a stouter sylvan hero elaborately accoutred for the chase. On more than one occasion this royal official had acted as go-between to the court and the Company; and in 1635, certain drainage projects of his on a royal grant of land in Lincolnshire having failed, he was on the look-out for some means of mending his fortunes.

The confederates, Courten, Pindar, and Porter, commanded a greater capital than the Company could then raise, and they wielded an influence with which it could not cope. In 1628 it had asked Parliament either to uphold it or to abolish the trade. Parliament had vouchsafed no answer, and the Company had ever since been wearying the king with tales of its losses. A trade so disastrous to its conductors could scarcely be profitable to the realm, within the meaning of the charter, especially when new capitalists were willing to take it up with more energy and spirit. The three allies formed the bold design of erecting themselves into a rival Company, with the king as their partner—a partner who should bring in no money, but earn his profits by his secret support.

Charles had a plain course open to him. He had only to give the East India Company the three years' notice required by the charter, and either resume its monopoly or force it to come to terms. Some of its members were quite ready for a compromise, and indeed preferred the "Regulated" system of separate ventures to a Joint Stock. Others were so despondent that they desired nothing better than to have three years allowed for bringing home their ships and property. In 1635 the king granted a license to his three friends on the ground that the Company had consulted only its own interests, neglected those of the nation, and broken the conditions on which its exclusive privileges had been bestowed. Instead, however, of giving the three years' notice Charles assured the Company that the new association would not trade within its jurisdiction, but was to "be employed on some secret design which his Majesty at present thought not fit to reveal."

In vain the dismayed governor waited in the Whitehall antechamber all forenoon. He only succeeded in thrusting a petition into the king's hand as his Majesty passed forth after dinner, but got not a word in reply. News soon arrived that two of Courten's ships which sailed "without any cargoes" almost as undisguised privateers, had plundered an Indian vessel in the Red Sea; and that the Company's servants at Surat were in prison for the piracy. Other of Courten's captains so outraged the Canton magistrates that the English were declared enemies of the Chinese Empire, and were to be for ever excluded from its ports. Projects by interlopers for plantations in Madagascar and the Mau-

THE OLD EAST INDIA HOUSE ON LEADENHALL STREET, 1726-1796.
After an old drawing.

ritius; armed settlements by Courten's agents on the Malabar coast; and their open hostility to the Company's servants at Surat and elsewhere now become the staple of the India Office records. The Company's factors in the East vainly begged for orders as to whether they were to obey the charter of King James, or the letters of King Charles which the newcomers flourished in their faces.

Charles had another chance given him. On Sir William Courten's death in 1636 his grant lapsed, and the king had only to enforce the three years' notice clause of the Company's charter in order to compel its despondent and wearied shareholders to a coalition. But his secret bonds forbade open methods, so he desired the Company not to trouble the dying man about the ships, and presently issued a new license to his son, William Courten, and his associates.

The remaining years of freedom left to Charles form a record of subterfuges to conceal his real relations to the rival companies. If the old Company arrested a servant of the new one for infringing its charter, the king did not defend him, but merely ordered his release. If the old Company by process of law stayed the interlopers' ships, his Majesty or the lords of his Council arranged to let them go. He was prodigal of good wishes to the directors, dangled wider privileges before their eyes, and pressed on them the good offices of his government to compose the disputes which his own action had stirred up. But their attendance on the Privy Council only resulted in royal rebukes delivered by the Archbishop of Canterbury, and reproaches from Lord Arundell.

The Company was in no humour to be harangued by Howard, or to be lectured by Laud. His Majesty's request that if the Earl of Southampton, "who is a noble and brave gentleman, shall make any offer or proposition to the Company" (needless to say for the brave gentleman's own benefit), "that they shall be pleased to hearken unto it," fell on deaf ears. The Company had tried his Majesty's courts in vain; it had tried his Majesty's Privy Council in vain; it had tried the king in person in vain. Slowly and very reluctantly it resolved once more to try the House of Commons.

Charles became afraid. The same need of money which had tempted him into a confederacy against the Company now compelled him to summon a Parliament. Within four days of its meeting in April, 1640, the Company was considering whether it should not lay its wrongs before the Commons. Mr. Recorder, however, counselled it not "to make his Majesty's proceedings notorious," and the abrupt dissolution of Parliament, after a three weeks' wrangle with the Crown, seemed to put an end to the project. The Company's stock fell so low that £100 of it sold for £60, as is shown by the entries of the Court Book. But in November of the same year the king, with a mutinous army and the Scotch war on his hands, was forced again to call together the estates of the realm. The Long Parliament met in wrath at the king's creatures, and promptly arrested Strafford. In January, 1641, the Company, feeling that it was once more on the flood-tide of popular feeling, petitioned Parliament against Courten and against Endymion Porter, his Majesty's groom of the bedchamber.

Charles in distress sent hurried messages to the governor of the Company to attend at Whitehall. The counsellors, on whose audacity he had relied, were themselves trembling; Strafford and Laud were impeached. Mr. Secretary Windebank and Lord Keeper Finch were soon to take flight, the Star Chamber and the Court of High Commission were doomed. The king at length confessed to the governor of the Company "that Mr. Porter had nothing to do in the business, his name only being used; that what was done was his Majesty's act." The petition, therefore, must not go forward. The governor feared it was too late: the petition had been delivered to the House on Friday night.

The king astutely replied that it was not too late, as the petition had not yet been read; and that he had in view a very fine thing for the Company, but that "without him they could never get a penny." With a spark of the royal spirit which flickered up in his worst distresses, Charles declared that if the petition were pressed he would publicly own that Porter was only a screen for himself. In the end the governor sent round to the House of Commons, recovered the petition, and begged the Company to believe he had acted for the best, although "as yet he durst not divulge the reasons thereof."

Charles was grateful for his escape. His thanks to the Company, and those of his groom of the bedchamber, were the prelude to a real effort to afford it redress. Courten supposed, however, that he still had the king secretly on his side, and insisted on terms which put an end to the negotiations. The Company now gave up further hopes from Charles. In June, 1641, it petitioned Parliament, and thenceforward boldly laid its grievances before the Commons.

But Parliament regarded the Company as the creation of the royal prerogative, and was by no means ardent on its behalf. It forbade the reprinting of the Amboyna Book against the Dutch, although Courten's

A SCENE IN THE BOMBAY PRESIDENCY, WESTERN INDIA.

"Red Sea Pyrate" captain was at length lodged in prison, in 1642. To the Commons, indeed, the Company seemed one of the secret sources of money which had helped Charles to do without their constitutional supplies. The Company now threw itself on their mercy, and in 1646 attempted to re-incorporate itself on a Parliamentary basis, under the form of an "Ordinance for the Trade," which practically re-affirmed the provisions of its royal charter. The Commons, after a good deal of money had been spent, agreed, and gave Courten three years to withdraw from India. But the House of Lords rejected the bill, in spite of the report of their own committee in its favour. The Company was at the end of its resources, and a new joint stock could not be raised. In 1646 the governor, in despair, advised the shareholders to "draw home their factors and estate," yet the court determined to go on for another year. In 1648 it resolved to abolish seven of its Indian factories.

The Company was a loyal body, but Charles wore out its loyalty. The fines and sequestrations afterwards laid on its stubbornly royalist members by Parliament and the Commonwealth fill many documents. Indeed, the sole great act of betrayal perpetrated by a servant of the Company was committed in the king's cause. Captain Mucknell treacherously carried his ship into Bristol, then held for his Majesty, and made her over for the support of the war against Parliament at a loss of £20,000 to his masters. It was a useless crime, and only added resentment to the directors' distrust of the king. Whatever his Majesty might say, the Company had always found that he left something unsaid, and that the royal prerogative, which he professed to exercise on its behalf, was at the secret service of its rivals.

Yet if these records disclose Charles I in an unheroic light, they also enable us to understand how he salved his own conscience. The kings of Portugal and of Spain had drawn large profits from the Indian trade, the King of France was about to try to do so, and why should Charles alone among the sovereigns of Europe deny himself? Nor is it by any means clear how far his early connivance with the opposition inside the Company, or with its "battulated" member, was his own act or that of the creatures about him. To force the Company to sell him its pepper, and then quickly to resell it at a loss without paying for it, would be called by an ill name in a modern law court. But the king had given bonds for the amount, and when they could not be realized, there is a pathos in his momentary earnestness to make restitution, even by the sale of the royal parks. When he violated the charter by a license to, and his secret partnership in, Courten's Association, he half-believed that he secured the Company from damage by the condition that the new adventurers should not trade to its disadvantage. India was surely wide enough for both, and the king fancied that he could partition the Indian markets between the two without loss to either.

To all this there is a plain answer. Charles was not an absolute monarch like the kings of Spain, or Portugal, or France, and his very twinges of conscience show that he knew it. Even if he had been an absolute sovereign, his father had limited the exercise of the royal prerogative by the charter granted to the Company. He might have withdrawn that charter by giving the three years' notice to the Company and firmly facing its opposition. But to this straightforward course

Charles could never make up his mind. Elizabeth, imperious, wayward, yet sensible, had maintained the royal prerogative of monopolies by surrendering its abuses. Under James I, a genuine although foolish person, that prerogative had received a rude shock; under Charles I it became a discredited legend. His high pretensions and low expedients wearied out the Company, as they had wearied out the nation; and the Company's appeal to Parliament was the commercial counterpart of the nation's appeal to the sword.

CHAPTER VI

FIRST ENGLISH SETTLEMENTS ON THE BOMBAY COAST

1607 - 1658

AMID the discomfitures and distresses of the Company at home, resolute groups of Englishmen were making their presence felt in India. The sites of their settlements were at first determined by political rather than by commercial considerations. During centuries the natural meeting-marts of the Indo-European spice trade had been the ports of Malabar; but the monopoly of those marts was secured to Portugal by her fortress-capital at Goa, and the coast rajas were on too small a scale to afford protection to newcomers. If our captains of the "Separate Voyages" were to find a footing in India, it must be under the shelter of a strong native government. The march of the Moghul Empire southwards, at the end of the sixteenth century, gave them their chance. Leaving the direct route from Africa to Malabar, they struck northeast to the Gulf of Cambay, on whose coasts the Moghul Emperor Akbar had imposed his rule, between 1572 and 1592.

Surat, the emporium of this ocean inlet and the capital of Gujarat, lies on a bend of the Tapti where the stream sweeps abruptly westward toward the sea. The name Surat is the modern representative of the ancient province of Surashtra, which at one time included not only Gujarat but part of Kathiawar. In ancient times the city was the chief maritime centre of India, and Ptolemy, about 150 B.C., speaks of the

A GENERAL VIEW OF SURAT.
After an old print.

trade of Pulipula, which has been identified with Phulpada, the old sacred part of Surat town. In course of time, however, the silt-bearing currents of its river and sand-laden ocean tides blocked its approach to mediæval shipping, although they formed a roadstead protected by mud-banks at Suwali, near the river mouth. Gujarat was cut off from the Moghul base in Northern India by mountains and deserts, and its annexation to the Moghul Empire cost twenty years of war, from 1572 to 1592. The work of conquest was rudely interrupted by revolts, which flared up afresh in the early years of the seventeenth century; but the long arm of the empire at length prevailed, and just as the anarchy ended the English came upon the scene.

In 1607, Captain William Hawkins, of the third "Separate Voyage," landed at Surat with a letter from James I to the Moghul Emperor Jahangir, and proceeded to the court at Agra. But the magnificent monarch of India did not take seriously the proffers of an unknown island-king brought by a ship's captain. Such European influence as then existed at the Moghul capital was entirely Portuguese; and, after four years, Hawkins returned to Surat with a native wife, but without any grant for trade. Meanwhile the local governor of Surat had allowed some of Hawkins's followers to remain there, apparently as a set-off to the Portuguese, who formed an unruly element at the roadstead. In 1609 a shipwrecked crew of our fourth "Separate Voyage" also claimed shelter. This the Moghul governor, whether "bribed by the Portugals" or merely afraid lest he should have too many of the European infidels on his hands, discreetly refused. The poor sailors had to make their way home, part of them by way of Lisbon, by the clemency of the Portuguese, who were only too glad to get rid of them.

The accounts which thus reached England from Surat, of its settled government under the *ægis* of the Great Moghul, and of its opportunities for trade, determined the Company to effect a settlement at its port. In 1611 Sir Henry Middleton, of the sixth "Separate Voyage," landed at Suwali in spite of the Portuguese, although they had compelled him to do business by exchanging cargoes in the roadstead. The Moghul governor, while still refusing us a factory, allowed some trade. Next year, 1612, Captain Best with the old *Red Dragon* and the little *Hosiander* routed the Portuguese squadron that commanded the approaches to Surat, while the Moghul governor looked on from the shore. A month's hard fighting destroyed for ever the Indian legend of the Portuguese supremacy over other Europeans. The gallant Captain Best would have been satisfied with his victory, but he had with him a man who was resolved that England should reap its full results. Thomas Aldworth, factor and merchant, improved the momentary congratulations of the Moghul governor into a grant for our first settlement in India.

"Through the whole Indies," Aldworth wrote to the Company in 1613, "there cannot be any place more beneficial for our country than this, being the only key to open all the rich and best trade of the Indies." With a handful of English merchants in an unfortified house he struggled through the reaction against us which followed the departure of Best's ships, until Downton's sea-fight two years later established for ever our superiority at Surat over the Portuguese.

Downton's feat of arms proved, unexpectedly, to be a great strategic victory. He had cut in half the Portuguese line of communication along the Indian coast. That line was held by Goa as its southern, and by Diu as its northern, base; and between the two by a squadron, which assured to Portugal the traffic of Surat and the Gulf of Cambay. This trade now passed to the English, and it became necessary to secure it by no mere grants of local Moghul governors, but by an in-

A VIEW IN THE CITY OF AJMIR.

strument from the Imperial Court. In January, 1615, while Downton was battering the Portuguese fleet off Surat, James I issued his commission to Sir Thomas Roe "to be ambassador to the Great Mogul," the

Company to pay all expenses and to reap any results that might accrue.

Roe reached Surat in September, 1615, and proceeded to the Moghul court, then at Ajmir. Surat was the chief starting-place for Mecca, and the Portuguese squadrons had troubled the ocean path of pilgrimage. The Imperial Court, too happy that one infidel fleet should destroy another, granted to Sir Thomas Roe an "Order" for trade. These "Orders" were sometimes called "grants" or "licenses," and sometimes dignified with the name of "treaties."[1] The truth is that as our power in India increased they gradually developed from mere permits into grants, then into treaties, and finally into *de jure* confirmations of conquests which

[1] Farmana, variously spelt Phirmaund, Firman, etc., in the Company's records. Under the strongly centralized system of the Moghul Empire every authorization, whether for succession to an office or to an estate, or for the levying of a toll, or for trade, or for industrial enterprises (from the manufacture of salt to the reclamation of waste lands and the cutting down of the jungle), required an order from the throne or its local representative. The word "treaty" is misapplied to such grants. From the native point of view they divide themselves into four not strictly demarcated classes. (1) *Parwānas*, permits issued by an executive officer, the governor of a port, or sometimes a mere custom house subordinate. (2) *Nishāns*, literally "signs," in the form of a sealed document, or flag, or other emblem, from the local authority of a district or province. (3) *Farmānas*, issued by the emperor or his viceroys or deputies. A farman was literally an "Order" conferring title, rank, command, office, or privileges, and was essentially of the nature of an imperial command. It had the wide sense which attaches to our term "Order," from a General Order in the Field to an Order in Council or a Local Government Order, or Order by the Board of Trade. (4) *Sanads*, or grants for land, money, inheritance, or high administrative office, under the Imperial seal, and serving as a discharge to the treasury for payments, allowances, or exemptions of revenue. The early servants of the Company in India had to content themselves with the inferior classes of permits, *parwānas* and *nishāns*; then followed *farmānas*, and finally *sanads*. But during their first century and a half in India, for "treaty" or "grant" it is generally safe to substitute the word "order."

we had *de facto* won. The treaty as drafted by Sir Thomas Roe would have allowed the English to found factories at all ports of the Moghul Empire, particularly in Gujarat, in Bengal, and in Sind; and exempted them from inland transit tolls, on payment of a fixed import duty of $3\frac{1}{2}$ per cent. on goods and 2 per cent. on treasure. But these proposals, although they figure as "Roe's Treaty" in Anglo-Indian histories, never passed beyond the draft stage and were rejected by the Imperial Court. Roe obtained, however, a permit for the English to reside at Surat and to travel freely into the interior, together with an order for the redress of the injuries inflicted on them by the local officials. He afterwards, in 1618, received a farman, or grant, in similar although somewhat handsomer terms, from the heir apparent, Prince Mirza Khurram, afterwards the Emperor Shah Jahan, then "fifteenth Viceroy of Gujarat," the province of which Surat was the chief port. The prince allowed the English to hire, although not to buy or build, a house for their trade at Surat, and promised the assistance of boats in case they were attacked by the Portuguese. Sir Thomas Roe lingered long enough among the Moghul grandees to find that he was by no means regarded as the ambassador of an equal sovereign. But his presence at the Imperial Court, and the heir apparent's viceroyalty of Gujarat, gave prestige to the English at Surat.

Meanwhile Captain Keeling, the "General" of the squadron which had brought out Roe, resolved to carry the war against the Portuguese into Southern India.

THE RUINED CITY OF SARKHAJ NEAR AHMADABAD.

Keeling was a sailor of taste with a wide outlook into the possibilities of his times. On a previous voyage, while detained at Sierra Leone, in September, 1607, he and his crew had played "Hamlet" and "Richard II" by way of private theatricals. He believed in India as a career, and wanted to carry his wife with him—but gave up his request on compensation of £200 from the Company. He now, in 1616, sailed boldly to Malabar, and tried to turn the flank of the southern Portuguese base at Goa, by a treaty with Calicut further down the coast. The allies were to drive out the Portuguese from Cochin, which was then to be made over to the English.

This project failed, but a halcyon period opened to the English at Surat. The crop-fields of Gujarat, with their miracle of two harvests a year, seemed a paradise to the storm-tossed mariners, as they rowed up the smooth channels of the Tapti. "Often of two adjoining fields," they wrote, "one was as green as a fine meadow, and the other waving yellow like gold and ready to be cut down." They might regret that spices did not grow so far north, but they found substitutes in the fine cotton fabrics and dyes of upper India. Small English agencies, which were thrown out into the interior (in Gujarat, Ahmadabad, Kathiawar—especially the Kathiawar coast of the Gulf of Cambay—and Sind), collected the muslins of the neighbouring provinces, and the indigo of Agra, for shipment at Surat.

The titular viceroyalty of the heir apparent to the

empire left the real administration of Gujarat in the hands of the governor who had seen us shatter the Portuguese fleet. Indeed the Emperor Jahangir complains in his "Memoirs" that this too liberal official bought from the Europeans a turkey and other curiosities quite regardless of the price.[1] An annalist makes the transaction take place at "Gogo" (Goa), in whose safe anchorage on the opposite side of the Cambay Gulf, our ships, when driven from the Suwali roadstead, could always find shelter. According to letters from India to the Company in 1616 and 1617, the only drawbacks to the Company's success at Surat were the "voluntaries," or private traders from England, who began to creep in, and who, when their speculations failed, became a burden on the factory, or turned Mohammedans "to keep them from starving."

More formidable rivals soon came upon the scene. In 1616 a Dutch ship under Van den Broeck appeared in the roadstead, but was not allowed to establish a factory. Next year two Dutch ships got wrecked off the coast, and ten of the survivors remained at Surat. In 1618 they received a license from the Moghul government, notwithstanding the efforts of Sir Thomas Roe to "turn them out," and in 1620 Van den Broeck re-

[1] The turkey seems to have been introduced into India by the Portuguese. Its present Hindustani name, *piru*, is identical with the Portuguese *peru*, derived from Peruana (Peru) in its old wider sense. Peruana and Guyana were used to denote Spanish-America at least as late as the almanacs of Charles II's reign; and the turkey, probably brought by Cortez to Spain, was long called the Guinea fowl. In Hindustani it preserves the other old name of Spanish-America, Peruana. Bluteau, in his *Vocabulario Portuguez e Latino*, 1720, gives no certain sound.

turned to Surat as director of Dutch trade. But the Dutch, accustomed to barbarian island chiefs, did not realize that they had come under an empire which insisted on good behaviour, and could crush the petty infidel settlements by a stroke of the pen. Even the English, backed by the imperial order for trade, had to rest satisfied with the protection assured to all residents within the Moghul Empire, and were not allowed to fortify their house at Surat. The Dutch attacks on native vessels now involved us in the common disgrace of the European name, and while the Dutch were slaughtering us at Amboyna, in 1623, the English at Surat were held responsible by the Moghul governor for the piracy of their most bitter enemies. He seized upon our warehouses, threw our president and factors into irons, and let them hold their consultations "in prison" for seven months, amid the revilings of "whole rabbles of people."

The Moghul government, however, soon learned to discriminate. It ceased, at any rate, to confound the peaceable English traders, who paid their customs punctually and abhorred images, with the Portuguese, who prostrated themselves like Hindus before a tinsel goddess, and plundered the True Believers on the holy voyage to Mecca. In 1622 our factory at Surat had organized the fleet which destroyed the Portuguese power in the Persian Gulf, and so outflanked the northern base of the Portuguese at Diu, which had controlled the entrance to the Gulf of Cambay. The English, having thus freed the approaches at Surat from the menace of the Portuguese, came to be regarded by the Moghul viceroy as a useful sea-police.

But the Portuguese, although beaten out of the Gulf of Cambay and the Persian Gulf, still harassed the route to the Red Sea. Surat was the main exit of the empire to Mecca, and the Moghul government hit upon the device of employing one nation of the infidels against another to keep open the pilgrim ocean highway. In 1629 it granted by a farman, or "order," letters of marque to our president at Surat to make reprisals on all Portuguese ships, whether at sea or in harbour. Next year a Surat governor again witnessed a repulse of the Portuguese from his river, "our English" driving the landing parties pell-mell into the sea, and "not fearing to run up to the chin in water, even to the frigates' sides." We rescued the viceroy's son in the sight of the whole people, "to their great admiration and our nation's great honour." In the following winter, December, 1630, the treaty of Madrid declared that thenceforth the English and Portuguese should dwell at peace in the Indies, and enjoy a free commerce open to both—a consummation not to be attained by parchment alliances.

The English at Surat thus early won for themselves a recognized position as trustworthy payers of revenue and as a maritime patrol for the Moghul Empire. On shore the empire was, within its limits, all powerful, but at sea it depended on mercenary fleets. As it held in check the pirate nests along the western shores of India by subsidizing the Abyssinian chiefs who had settled on that coast, so it looked to the English at Surat to keep open the ocean path of pilgrimages to the holy cities of the Red Sea. The Moghul supremacy was essentially of land origin. It had started from Central Asia, spread from the mountain passes across the Panjab, forced its way through the Aravalli deserts to Gujarat, and followed the courses of two mighty rivers, the Indus and the Ganges, to the opposite shores of India. From the vast hinterland of Hindustan the Moghul emperors were constrained to find an outlet to the ocean. But the great distance of their capitals in Northwestern India from the coast rendered it impossible, when they had found an outlet, to exercise an effective sea-control.

On the east, Portuguese buccaneers and Arakanese pirates swept the Bay of Bengal, and the Moghul viceroy had, by a special tax, to maintain an armed flotilla to keep open the mouths of the Ganges. On the west, the royal galleons and frigates of Portugal blocked the approaches to the Indus and the Gulf of Cambay. What the river fleet of the Bengal viceroy did for the Gangetic delta, the Indian emperors resolved that the English at Surat should do for the Arabian Ocean. Our squadrons formed, in fact, the naval complement to the land-conquest of Gujarat by the Moghul Empire. The anarchy which had ended just as we arrived gave place to a period of prosperity unexampled in the history of the province. Caravans came and went to all the inland capitals of India—Golkonda, Agra, Delhi, Lahore; the products of Asia, from the Straits of Malacca to the Persian Gulf, were piled up on the wharves of the Tapti. Merchants flocked in such numbers to Surat that during the busy winter months lodgings could scarcely be had. A succession of able men directed the English factory; and soon after 1616 a Surat chaplain, Henry Lord, commenced those liberal researches into the native customs and religions, which are among the most honourable memorials of our Indian rule, and

A NATIVE VESSEL IN THE STRAITS OF MALACCA.

which have done much to mould that rule to the needs of the people.

The Company saw the position which its little band of servants had won on the Gulf of Cambay, and recognized the president at Surat as the chief of the English in India. After Amboyna the hopes of reviving the trade in the Spice Archipelago flickered out, and in 1630 even Bantam, its headquarters in Java, was declared subordinate to Surat. In the same year a calamity fell upon Gujarat which enables us to realize the terrible meaning of the word famine in India under native rule. Whole districts and cities were left bare of inhabitants.

In 1631 a Dutch merchant reported that only eleven of the 260 families at Suwali survived. He found the road thence to Surat covered with bodies decaying "on the highway where they died, [there] being no one to bury them." In Surat, that great and crowded city, he "could hardly see any living persons;" but the corpses "at the corner of the streets lie twenty together, nobody burying them." Thirty thousand had perished in the town alone. Pestilence followed famine. The president and ten or eleven of the English factors fell victims, with "divers inferiors now taken into Abraham's bosom"—three-fourths of the whole settlement. "No man can go in the streets without giving great alms or being in danger of being murdered, for the poor people cry aloud, 'Give us sustenance, or kill us.'" "This, that was in a manner the garden of the world, is turned into a wilderness."

The Dutchman estimated that it would take three years before the trade could revive at Surat. Indeed, one striking contrast between native and British rule was the slowness of recovery from famine in the Moghul Empire. But the English at Surat clung to the wreck of their settlement, and their new jurisdiction over our other factories in India placed at their command the whole of the Company's ships in the Indian seas. A strong naval force thus came under the centralized control of Surat. The Company had from twenty to twenty-five vessels employed in the East Indies, chiefly in port to port trade. In 1629, it declared that during the past twelve years it had "sent out fifty-seven ships containing 26,690 tons, besides eighteen pinnaces, to be worn out by trading from port to port in The Indies."

To this scattered fleet, strongly armed and always eager to fight, the Surat factory added a local flotilla of stout sea-going craft, carrying two to six guns apiece, and charged with the defence of the Tapti estuary and Gulf of Cambay. Ten of these Surat "grabs and gallivats" are said to have existed in 1615, during Captain Downton's six weeks' battle with the Portuguese, and from that year the permanent establishment of our Indian navy has been reckoned. In 1622, four of them accompanied the squadron which drove the Portuguese from Ormuz and the Persian Gulf. These Surat cruisers were greatly superior to the Portuguese "frigates." Yet the Portuguese "frigates" sufficed to make it unsafe for Dutch ships to lie in at the Malabar roadsteads. The broad lateen sails, light draught, and hardy rowers of the Surat "grabs," or galleys, enabled them to outmanœuvre both the Dutch and the Lisbon galleons along the shore. When combined with the heavily armed English ships engaged in the port to port trade, they made up a formidable force.

The viceroy at Goa now found his whole line of communication on the west coast of India dominated by our Surat factory. The English at Surat, on their side, felt the necessity for a direct trade with the pepper districts and spice ports of Malabar, which also remained the Indian marts of exchange for the more precious cloves and nutmegs of the Eastern Archipelago. European diplomacy had failed to secure peace between the Christian nations in Asia. So, in 1634, the Viceroy of Goa and the English president at Surat took the matter into their own hands and entered into direct negotiations. They signed a formal truce, which in 1635 they

A TEAK-WOOD HOUSE AT SURAT.

developed into a commercial convention on the basis of the ineffective Madrid treaty of 1630. Two English ships were annually to obtain a cargo at Goa, two more might load at other Portuguese factories. The long promised *liberum commercium* between the English and Portuguese in India became an accomplished fact.

It was this talent of isolated groups of Englishmen for making their power felt in distant regions, that carried the Company through the dark days of Charles I. They turned their factory at Surat into a sea-defence of the Moghul Empire, convoyed noble and imperial devotees to the Persian Gulf on their way to Mecca, and guarded the pilgrim route. Their Dutch rivals, although much stronger in men and ships in Asiatic waters, found themselves on the Gujarat coast in the grip of the Moghul power. Nor did the Hollanders, secure of the Spice Archipelago, care so much to come to terms with the Indian Portuguese.

But while our Surat factors thus secured a strong position and earned large profits for their masters, they also, in spite of their masters, did a lucrative trade on their own account. The Company viewed with mixed emotions the rising power of its servants in the East. It had seen its president at Surat commission a squadron in 1628 to wage open war on the Portuguese. But for a local factory to make a treaty on its own account with an independent European power was a dangerous audacity. Yet, in 1636, in spite of the home directors' alarm and half-heartedness, this convention of the Goa viceroy with the president at Surat became the basis of the settlement of the Indies.

Even Holland began to realize that, notwithstanding her Spice Island supremacy, the English understood the greater game of Indian politics better than her own servants in the East. The Dutch factors at Surat contrasted their insignificance with the strong position which the English, by the favour of the Moghul sovereign, enjoyed. In a letter from Surat to the governor-general at Batavia, April 30, 1634, they wrote: "We have no real power in these countries," they lament, "while the (Moghul) governors can always revenge any real or pretended affront, by laying an embargo on the Company's property." The truth is that the Dutch governors-general at Batavia, domineering over their petty island chiefs, had the very worst training for the direction of distant factories under the irresistible Moghul emperors. "The English get daily a firmer footing in India," "we should act in concert with the English," "a good understanding with the English is the best guarantee of our commerce in India" – the Dutch factors at Surat reiterated in vain.

From their height of prosperity the handful of English at Surat were suddenly cast down. In 1636 arrived Captain Weddell of Courten's Association, with a letter from King Charles to our president, intimating that under his Majesty's authority six ships "had been sent on a voyage of discovery to the South Seas," and that "the king himself had a particular interest" in the expedition. Presently came news that two of these ships "to the South Seas" had turned pirates in the Red Sea and plundered an Indian vessel. The Moghul governor at once seized our factory at Surat, threw the president and Council into prison for two months, and only released them on payment of 170,000 rupees, or about £18,000, and on their solemn oath (in spite of their protestations of innocence) never again to molest a Moghul ship.

As in 1623 the Moghul government had held the Company's servants responsible for the piracy of their public enemies the Dutch, so in 1636 it punished them for the piracy of Courten's interlopers. "Wee must beare the burthen," says a sorrowful despatch quoted by Anderson, "and with patience sitt still, until we may find these frowning tymes more auspicious to us and to our affayres."

A still heavier blow was about to fall on the poor prisoners at Surat. While the piracies of Courten's Association brought them into disgrace with the Moghul government, the ablest captain of the interlopers, Weddell, resolved to snatch the fruits of the Surat president's convention with the Portuguese viceroy. He sailed to Goa, and, on the strength of a letter from King Charles, got leave in 1637-1638 to hire a house and to land his goods. After forcing himself, by the same authority, on the Company's struggling factories from the Bay of Bengal to near the Straits of Malacca, he fixed his headquarters at Rajapur on the Bombay coast. The site was well chosen. It lay up a long tidal creek, in the independent kingdom of Bijapur, about half-way between Goa and the modern city of Bombay. It thus cut in two the Company's line of communication between Surat and Goa, as the Company's settlement at Surat had cut in two the Portuguese line of communication between Goa and Diu. The Moghul Empire had not then advanced so far down the coast, and Raja-

ENCAMPING AT RAJAPUR NEAR THE BOMBAY COAST.

From Rousselet's India.

pur formed a chief inlet of the Arabian commerce for the yet unconquered kingdoms of the South. In vain the Company's servants at Surat protested and tried to found a rival station in the South. Captain Weddell secured by lavish gifts the support of the King of Bijapur, and began to plant factories along the coast. The sagacity of his selection is proved by the part which these factories played in the subsequent annals of the Company.

From home the Surat factory could get no succour, nor any certain sound from their distracted masters, then in their desperate struggle with the court cabal. We have seen that fifty-seven ships and eighteen pinnaces had been sent out for port to port trade alone, during the twelve years ending 1629. The Company's records, which during the same period abound in journals of voyages to and from India, preserve only eight such documents for the thirteen disastrous years from King Charles's grant to Courten's Association in 1635 to his Majesty's death in 1649.

But the factors of the Company at Surat, although left to ruin, asserted their vitality in a wholly unexpected manner. They practically kept up the trade on their own account, continued to patrol the pilgrim highway, and maintained an attitude at once so reasonable and so resolute that the Moghul government repented of having punished them for the piracy of their rivals.

As the emperor used the English to check the piracy of the Portuguese, so he employed them to bring it to an end. The Portuguese had continued to plunder Moghul ships, subject to such reprisals as the English could inflict on them. But the English president at Surat had now made a treaty on his own account with the Goa viceroy: Why should he not also include in it the Indian government? In 1639 the Surat Council found themselves raised into negotiators between the Moghul governor and the Portuguese. The degenerate successors of Albuquerque and the half-breed corsairs of Goa for a time transferred their piracies from the Mecca route to the Bay of Bengal, and the cold shadows which had fallen on the Surat factory were again warmed into prosperity under the sunshine of the Moghul court. However low the fortunes of the Company sank under king or Commonwealth in England, the Surat factory grew with a strength of its own. In 1657, on account of the prosperous condition of that factory, the Company decided that there should be but one presidency in India—and that Surat.

I have narrated at some length the rise of the Surat factory for several reasons. It formed the first headquarters of the English in India—a centre of English control in the East which had a vitality in itself apart from the Company in London, and which won by its Persian Gulf victory our first revenue grant—the Customs of Gombroon—and profoundly influenced our later settlements on the Indian continent. It also illustrates the position which the English quickly secured in the economy of the Moghul Empire: as a sure source of revenue, a sea-police for the coast, and the patrol of the ocean path to Mecca, gradually developing into negotiators on behalf of the native government. Surat forms the type of an early English settlement under the strong hand of the Moghul emperors.

A SOUTHERN INDIAN SWORD.

CHAPTER VII

FIRST ENGLISH SETTLEMENTS ON THE MADRAS COAST

1611 - 1658

THE problem which lay before the English on the east coast of India was a more complex one. The Moghul Empire had not yet reached those distant shores. Instead of the firm order which it imposed on its provinces, the conflict of dynasties and races still raged. The inland Moslem kings of Golkonda advanced their boundaries to the Madras coast after the destruction of the Hindu suzerainty of Vijayanagar at the battle of Talikot in 1565. But the remnants of that ancient Hindu dynasty had sought refuge, and again gathered strength, in its eastern maritime provinces. There, backed by the shore rajas, its feudatories in more prosperous times, the descendants of the Hindu overlords still disputed with the Golkonda Moslems the hill tracts, the river deltas, and tidal lagoons.

The Madras coast looked out toward the Eastern Archipelago as the Bombay coast looked out toward Africa and the Cape. The Portuguese, advancing eastwards from their African base, formed their first and most lasting settlements on the Bombay side; the Dutch, reverting westwards from their Spice Island dominions, established themselves chiefly on the Bay of Bengal. In 1609 they obtained a settlement at Pulicat, a long, low isle with the surf breaking on its outer

MADRAS.

shores, and a sheltered lagoon stretching inwards to the mainland, about twenty-three miles north of Madras city. Its great backwater, or "Pulicat Lake," formed by the sea bursting through the sand-dunes of the coast in some ancient cyclonic storm, afforded a haven for the shipping of those days.

In 1611 Captain Hippon and Peter Floris in *The Globe* of our seventh Separate Voyage essayed a landing at Pulicat. Floris was a Hollander who had learned the secrets of the Indian trade while in the Dutch service. Captain Hippon, with the knowledge thus obtained, resolved to strike into the port to port trade, which bartered the calicoes of the Madras coast for the spices of the Eastern Archipelago. Not unnaturally, the Dutch, who had meanwhile built a fort at Pulicat, "did beare a hard hand against them." The queen of the place refused even to see our captain, saying that a grant had already been given to the Hollanders. But Hippon, although cast down, was not dismayed. He sailed further up the coast, and landed at Pettapoli (the modern Nizampatam), at the mouth of a southern channel of the Kistna delta—more exposed to the monsoon than Pulicat, yet sufficiently sheltered for a ship to ride out a storm. There he arrived on August 18, 1611, was well received by the local governor, and left two supercargoes to found our first shore settlement on the Bay of Bengal. Of its fortunes presently.

In 1614 another captain of the English Company cast longing eyes on Pulicat. The Dutch "Rector of all the factories upon that coast" and his lieutenant, who was "English-born," feasted the visitors in their "castle," but firmly refused to let them trade. The Anglo-Dutch treaty of 1619 at length gave us this right, and at the same time compelled us to pay half the charges of the garrison. A band of English factors accordingly landed at Pulicat in 1620, and for a year their trade went "roundly forward." But the Dutch opposition, which was to culminate in the tragedy of

Amboyna, soon rendered our position untenable at Pulicat, and in 1623, shortly after that tragedy, we had to quit the lagoon-haven for a refuge further north. Later English projects to reoccupy Pulicat came to nothing, and our first attempt at a settlement on the Madras coast ended in failure and a heavy loss.

The mud-creeks of Pettapoli, where Captain Hippon had found shelter in 1611, promised, under the protection of the powerful Golkonda kings, a better fortune. In 1614 Peter Floris built a half-fortified factory at Pettapoli with a lofty flagstaff. But its mangrove-swamps were deadly, the trade was small, and the factory was dissolved in 1621; a solitary merchant being left to collect country cloths from the fever-stricken delta of the Kistna. In 1633 the English again settled at Pettapoli, and the factory lingered on to 1687, when it was finally broken up by orders from home. What the Dutch were to us at Pulicat the pestilence proved to us at Pettapoli. A local writer in the records of Fort St. George, Madras, in 1687 describes the whole region as depopulated and the trade "wholly ruined," "there being scarce people left to sow and reap their little harvest."

Thus perished our first two settlements on the Madras coast. But Captain Hippon, although he sought shelter at Pettapoli in 1611, seems to have suspected its unhealthiness, and after a halt sailed a few days northward, to Masulipatam. This ancient port (whose name, Masuli-patanam, or Machli-patanam, meant "Fish-town," and whose harbour is still known as Machlibandar, "Fishport") lay north of the great projection of fen-lands and mud-banks formed by the mouths of the Kistna (as Pettapoli lay to the south) and was to that extent better protected from the monsoon. Around it stretched a dreary expanse of sand, flooded into swamps during the months of the rains. To seawards, silt-bars and sand deposits make it unsafe for large modern ships to anchor within five miles of the shore,

A LANDING AT MASULIPATAM.

and from October to December the monsoon often renders it unapproachable. Yet it formed a coveted roadstead on the open coast-line of Madras, and became the scene of bitter rivalries—English, Dutch, and French. Its earliest surviving tombstone commemorates the "Chief by Water and by Land of the Dutch India Company on the Coromandel Coast. Died August 29, 1624." A later but more romantic memorial of the English settlers long shaded their dusty evening drive, and was known as "Eliza's Tree;" after Sterne's

"Eliza" (more strictly "Elizabeth" Sclater, or Mrs. Draper), who here solaced an uncongenial Indian marriage by a sentimental correspondence with the author of "Tristram Shandy." The tree itself was washed away by the cyclone wave of 1864.

On August 31, 1611, Captain Hippon and his Dutch lieutenant, Peter Floris, cast anchor at Masulipatam, loaded up *The Globe* with the local calicoes, and sailed eastwards to exchange them for spices at Bantam and the rich products of Siam. They left behind a few Englishmen to collect more "white cloths" pending their return. From that date an English trade went on; at first between Masulipatam and Sumatra or Java, but gradually throwing out offshoots along the Bay of Bengal, and eventually doing business with Surat and direct with England. Masulipatam was the chief seaport of the Moslem kings of Golkonda, who were not subdued by the Moghul Empire until 1687. It formed the outlet for the Golkonda diamonds and rubies, for the marvels of textile industry which had developed under the fostering care of that luxurious inland court, and for the commoner "white cloths" woven on the coast. The profits from their barter for the gold, camphor, benzoin ("benjamin"), and spices of the Eastern Archipelago and Siam were immense. In 1627 our council at Batavia recommended their Honourable Masters in London to send out each year £67,500 in specie to Masulipatam to be invested in country cloths, which would be exchanged in Batavia for spices at a profit of £135,000.

In Masulipatam the English found a half-way mart between the West and the Far East, scarcely less lucrative than the Portuguese seats of the Indo-European trade on the Malabar coast. We thus turned the eastern flank of the Portuguese in Southern India, as our Surat factory had turned the western flank of the Portuguese in Northern India and the Persian Gulf. But from the first, or almost from the first, our captains had to struggle with the Dutch for Masulipatam. The inland court of Golkonda, however, knew the advantages of keeping the port open to all comers, and here as at Surat the English seem to have understood the greater game of Indian politics better than their Dutch rivals accustomed to trample upon island chiefs. In 1613 the English obtained a grant for a fortified factory, "written on a leaf of gold," from the Hindu authorities in the interior—although not yet from the Golkonda kings; while the Dutch made the local governor their friend. Next year the English felt strong enough to give a severe lesson to this petty magnate, who seems to have been unpopular in his own city. As he refused to pay a sum of money due to them, they seized his son and, in their own words, "carried him aboard our ship prisoner in spite of one thousand of his people, to the Company's benefit, the honour of our king and country, and to the great content of all the Moors." Soon afterwards the local governor was dismissed and heavily fined, while the English obtained leave to trade at Masulipatam as freely as the Dutch or any other nation. "No factory in India," says a report in 1619, "hath been so fortunate and thrifty."

But the control of Golkonda over its distant provinces was very different from the firm grasp of the Moghul Empire. We must bear in mind that the old Hindu rulers, whom the Golkonda kingdom displaced, still exercised an authority on the coast; and it was from them and not from the Golkonda court that we received our first grants at Masulipatam. The confusion was scarcely less wild than the scramble of rival native claimants on the same coast, into which the English and the French plunged a century later. The retreat of a rebel son of the Moghul emperor through the district in 1624 added to the disorder. The Dutch again won over the local governor, who made our position "insufferable." Unable to resist or revenge his "foul injuries," our factors resolved in despair to abandon Masulipatam. They declared they would never return except under a grant from the King of Golkonda direct. On September 27, 1628, they stole out of their factory, leaving all behind, and secretly set off in a small boat for Armagon.

Their hard experiences in that wild roadstead further down the coast, I shall presently relate. In 1630, finding it impossible to collect a sufficient supply of the "white cloths" at Armagon, they crept back to Masulipatam. They returned to a city silenced by death, with no one either to help or hinder them. The great famine which desolated Surat had stretched across the whole Indian continent. At Masulipatam, our returned factors reported that "the major part of weavers and washers are dead and the country almost ruinated." "The living were eating up the dead, and men durst scarcely travel in the country for fear they should be killed and eaten."

As the final annexation of Gujarat to the Moghul Empire had put an end to anarchy on the northwestern coast of India and enabled the English to settle securely at Surat, so the gradual establishment of the Golkonda Mussulman dynasty on the east coast gave us an assured position at Masulipatam. In both cases we commenced with permits from subordinate coast authorities, and were eventually forced to seek a guarantee from the inland sovereign power.

What the prince imperial's grant to Sir Thomas Roe had been to our Surat factory, the "Golden Phirmaund" of the King of Golkonda in 1632 proved to the English settlement at Masulipatam. "Under the shadow of Me, the King, they shall sit down at rest and in safety." In return, our factors engaged to import Persian horses for his Majesty of Golkonda. Next year they were strong enough to send out a trading party northwards to attempt a settlement in Bengal. The importance of the Masulipatam factory declined on the growth of the more southern settlement which it founded at Madras in 1639. But in spite of the confusions arising from the struggle of the coast rajas with the inland kingdom of Golkonda, and of the subsequent collapse of Golkonda itself beneath the advancing power of the Moghul Empire, Masulipatam remained, and still remains, an important seat of Indo-European trade.

Armagon, the roadstead in which the fugitive factors from Masulipatam sought shelter in 1628, lay a few days' sail down the coast, and about forty miles north of our first attempted settlement at Pulicat. Armagon now figures as "a shoal and lighthouse" on modern charts, and its port, locally known as Durgarayapatnam, or Durgarazpatanam, is but a poor village

TOMBS OF THE KINGS OF GOLKONDA.

with some solar salt-pans and no commerce. In 1626 the English council at Batavia had obtained leave from the petty coast chief at Armagon to erect a factory. The flight of our factors from Masulipatam, two years later, made Armagon, miserable as it was, our sole shelter on the east coast. Resolved to hold it to the last, they landed twelve cannons from passing ships, and formed themselves into a small militia of twenty-three soldiers and merchants, against "the depredations of the natives and of the Dutch"—our first fortified garrison in India. But the place was too poor for aught save a temporary refuge. Country cloths could not be bought in sufficient quantity. Most of our factors flitted back to Masulipatam in 1630, and Armagon was practically abandoned for a new settlement further south in 1639. Again the Company lost, in the end, the outlay on buildings and fortifications.

The new settlement was Madras. In 1639 Francis Day, a member of the Masulipatam council and Chief at Armagon, proposed to get free of the struggle with the Dutch by founding a factory to the south of their Pulicat settlement. He discovered the place he wanted, thirty miles down the coast from Pulicat, with a practicable roadstead, and a friendly Portuguese colony on shore. The local Hindu chief welcomed the English and obtained for them from his inland raja (the descendant of the once great Hindu suzerains of Vijayanagar) a grant for a piece of land on the shore and the right to build a fort. The local chief piously directed that the new settlement should be called after his father, Chennappa, and to this day the natives know it by the name Chennapatanam; but the English called it Madras, probably from a Hindu shrine or legend of the place.

Without waiting for permission from home, Day built an embrasured factory and christened it Fort St. George in honour of England. The Company, uneasy about the money already sunk in fortified factories on the Madras coast, viewed the new settlement as another hazardous experiment, but left the council at Surat to decide whether it should go forward. The Surat council realized the advantages of a stronghold on the Bay of Bengal as a half-way house for the trade with Java, and gave their sanction. But six years later the Company at home had not forgiven its servants at Madras for the new expenses into which they had plunged. In 1645 it summoned one of them before its court "to answer the charge of the building of Fort St. George." It let him off only on the ground that "it was the joint act of all the factors;" and "if it should not prove so advantageous for the Company hereafter, it can be charged upon no man more justly than upon Mr. Day."

The little isolated group of Englishmen meanwhile pushed on the works, and, in spite of their Honourable Masters, founded the future capital of Southern India. The first General Letter from Fort St. George, dated November 5, 1642, announced that the chief settlement on the Coromandel coast had been transferred from Masulipatam to Madras. It humbly tried to argue away the displeasure of the Company at home, but with little success, for by 1644 the cost of the fortifications had mounted up to £2294; and it was found that another £2000 with a garrison of a hundred men would be required.

The Madras grant gave us our first piece of Indian soil, apart from the mere plots on which our factories were built. It was but a narrow strip running about a mile inland for six miles up the shore, north of the Portuguese monastic village that clustered around the shrine of Saint Thomé, or Saint Thomas, referred to in the preceding volume. It contained, however, a little island formed by two channels of the Cooum backwater —a swampy tidal patch, about four hundred yards long by one hundred broad, which could be defended against the attacks of predatory horsemen. Mr. Day built a wall round this river-girt ait, with a fort in its northern corner, and laid out the enclosure in lanes or alleys. As only Europeans were allowed to live within the walled isle, it became known as White Town, while the weaving hamlets which grew up outside, under the shelter of its guns, were called Black Town. The whole was included under the name of Madras.

The English had from the first secured their position by grants from the superior inland kings, while the Dutch preferred the facile support of the petty coast rulers, who more resembled their island chiefs in the Spice Archipelago. An English merchant penetrated to Golkonda as early as 1617, and in 1634 the importance was recognized of keeping "a continual residence" there, in order "to have an able man at all times so near the king's elbow." In 1645 the sovereign of Golkonda renewed the grant for Madras, and thus gained the good-will of our young settlement in his struggle with the feudal fragments of the Vijayanagar Empire. But two years later a terrible famine added to the calamities of the perpetual war between the Moslem Court of Golkonda and the Hindu coast chiefs. Trade came to an end, and our Surat factory had to send round a ship with provisions to save the Madras settlement from starvation. The Golkonda king, perhaps struck by such a display of distant resources, became eager for a closer alliance. In 1650 - 1651 he even proposed to form a Joint Stock with the English Company for trading between the ports of his kingdom and those of other Indian powers.

This dangerous honour, like the proffered partnership of James I, was prudently evaded. But the Com-

CAR OF THE GOD VITOBA AT VIJAYANAGAR.

pany in London perceived that a new future had opened for it on the Bay of Bengal. Hitherto Madras ranked as a subordinate agency to Bantam in Java. In 1653 it was raised to an independent presidency. Presently the Honourable Masters at home, in terrible straits to maintain their position from day to day, took fright at the cost of its new fortified factory, and in 1654 reduced the staff at Madras to two factors, with ten soldiers for their guard. The native powers at once detected this change of front; the Dutch, with superior forces on sea and land, seized upon the trade; and English interlopers flocked to the Madras roadstead. Then the Company, its courage revived by Cromwell's charter of 1657, resolved to make Madras its effective headquarters in Eastern India, and in 1658 declared all its settlements in Bengal and the Coromandel coast subordinate to Fort St. George. Thenceforward Madras stood as the type of the system of fortified factories, which the conflicts of the native powers in South-eastern India rendered indispensable for the safety of European trade.

CHAPTER VIII

FIRST ENGLISH SETTLEMENTS ON THE BENGAL COAST

1633 - 1658

IN Northwestern India the English had adapted themselves to the settled order of the Moghul Empire and won an honourable position as a coast-police and the patrol of the pilgrim ocean highway. In Southeastern India they had secured their settlements by grants from the inland kings, and by forts, amid the perpetual struggle between those kings and their half-subdued coast rajas. In Bengal they were to be confronted by a different set of political conditions.

The great satrapy of the Lower Ganges, including Bengal Proper and Orissa, was in itself so affluent, and lay so far from the Imperial Court, as to render it almost a separate sovereignty. Only by long wars, and after repeated revolts, had it been completely annexed to the Moghul Empire. When the Afghan kings of Bengal went down before the Emperor Akbar in 1576, they found a refuge in the adjoining province of Orissa. The slow subjugation of this dynasty, amid its hill-fastnesses and network of rivers, I have narrated in a work on the history of Orissa and its condition under British rule.

The Moghul governors who succeeded the Afghan

rulers were so remote from the Imperial control that they could oppress on their own account; yet at the same time could call in the whole force of the empire to crush resistance to their oppression. This semi-independence of the Ganges viceroys dominated our position in Bengal. It was a personal element which the Imperial Court kept under strict subjection in its nearer province of Gujarat. But it influenced our whole history on the Bengal seaboard, from our first gracious reception in Orissa, to the caprices of the half-mad youth infamous for the Black Hole of Calcutta.

The popular story of our settlement in Bengal is a pretty one. A patriotic ship-surgeon, Mr. Gabriel Boughton, having cured an imperial princess of a severe burn in 1636, would take no fee for himself, but secured for his countrymen the right to trade free of duties in Bengal. It is true that Mr. Boughton obtained an influence at the Moghul Court, but he did not go there until 1645, and meanwhile the English had fixed themselves on the Bengal seaboard by no romance of Imperial favour, but by sufferings and endurance of a deeper pathos.

The draft-treaty proposed by Sir Thomas Roe in 1616 had mentioned the ports of Bengal as places free to the English, and visions of trade with that distant province flitted before the Company's servants of Surat. Bengal was to be opened to them, however, not by any plunge of the Surat Council into the Eastern *terra incognita*, but by the gradual advance of the English up the Madras coast. The "Golden Phirmaund" (farman) of the Golkonda king in 1632 encouraged the Masulipatam factory to send a trading party northward. Accordingly in March, 1633, eight Englishmen started in a native "junk," "with a square sail, an oar-like rudder, and a high poop with a thatched house built on it for a cabin," and rolled up the Bay of Bengal till they reached the mouths of Mahanadi, literally the "Great River" of Orissa.

There, on April 21st, Easter Day, 1633, they cast

A NATIVE BOAT OF THE BAY OF BENGAL.

anchor inside the mud-banks of the Moghul customs-station of Harishpur on one of the tributaries of the Mahanadi River. The Hindu port-officer or "Rogger" (our sea-captain's rendering of raja) behaved with Indian courtesy to the strangers. But presently, as we know from the account by the ship's captain, William Bruton, which was published at London five years later, a Portuguese frigate steered into the haven, anchored close to our half-decked boat, and got up a scuffle on shore, "where our men being oprest by multitudes had like to have been all slaine or spoyled, but that

Lucklip the Rogger [*i. e.* Lakshmi the raja] rescued them with two hundred men."

Ralph Cartwright, the chief merchant, leaving the boat in the joint protection of its crew and the friendly port-officer, proceeded with a small deputation inland to the Moslem Governor of Orissa at Cuttack, at the delta-head of the Mahanadi, or Great River. Their mission was to "the Nabob of Bengal," but our simple explorers looked on one native ruler as much the same as another, and they thought that the governor of Orissa would serve their purposes equally well. The kindness which they met with on their few days' journey up the delta—kindness which Hindu hospitality showed to any stranger from a distant land who came in peace—impressed them deeply. The imposing etiquette of the court at Cuttack quickly brought them back to a sense of their position.

The Moslem Governor of Orissa was Agha Muhammad Zaman, who was born in Tahran, the capital of Persia. This distinguished soldier and able administrator was merely a deputy of the Moghul Viceroy of Bengal, but he was a polite Persian and knew how to combine courtesy with state, displaying a certain simplicity, half-military, half-religious. By day the lord of a magnificent palace, at night he slept like a soldier in his tent, "with his most trusty servants and guards about him," as we are told in Captain Bruton's "Newes from the East Indies" (published in 1638), from which this quotation and those in the next two paragraphs are taken. The gracious governor received the three Englishmen in his Hall of Public Audience amid Oriental splendour; affably inclined his head to Mr. Cartwright; then slipping off his sandal, offered "his foot to our merchant to kiss, which he twice refused to do, but at last he was fain to do it." Cartwright presented his gifts. Before, however, he could finish his petition for trade, "the king's almoner" gave the signal for prayer, the glittering court knelt down with their faces to the setting sun, and business ended for the day. Meanwhile the palace had been lighted up with a blaze of countless tapers, and the English returned to the quarters assigned to them in the adjacent city of Cuttack.

The picturesque negotiations which followed read like a tale out of the "Arabian Nights." Cartwright came with two distinct objects: redress for the Portuguese attack within a Moghul harbour, and a license for trade. The Portuguese captain lodged a counter-complaint against our crew, and each of the litigants purchased the aid of powerful officials. Cartwright asserted his title to seize the frigate on the bold ground "that all such vessels as did trade on the coast and had not a pass either from the English, Danes, or Dutch, were lawful prize." The Portuguese captain could produce only a pass from his own nation, which availed nothing, as the Moghul government looked on the Portuguese as pirates, and had in the preceding autumn, October, 1632, sacked their chief settlement in Bengal. Accordingly the governor "made short work with the matter, and put us all out of strife presently; for he confiscated both vessel and goods all to himself." This was too much for the English temper. To the astonishment of the courtiers "our merchant rose up in great anger and departed, saying that if he could not have right here, he would have it in another place. And so went his way, not taking his leave of the Nabob or of any other. At which abrupt departure they all admired."

The governor, rather amused than offended by his audacity, gave him three days to cool down, and then ordered him into the Presence. Cartwright knew that his life and those of his companions depended on a nod from the State Cushion. Yet "with a stern undaunted countenance" he declared that his Highness "had done his masters of the Honourable Company wrong, and by his might and power had taken their rights from them, which would not be so endured." This was a new language to the polite Persian. He inquired of the Indian merchants before him what sort of a nation it was that bred a man like that. They answered that it was a nation whose ships were such that no "vessel great or small" could stir out "of his Majesty's dominions; but they would take them." "At these words the king said but little, but what he thought is beyond my knowledge to tell you."

The result soon appeared. The governor or "King" kept the Portuguese frigate, but on May 5, 1633, he sealed an order giving the English an ample license to trade. It was addressed to "Ralph Cartwright, merchant," and granted him the liberty to traffic and export, free of customs, at any port of Orissa, and to purchase ground, erect factories, and build or repair ships. We had now, by the circuit of the Indian coast, re-entered the provinces of the Moghul Empire, and there was no question of fortifications, as on the unsettled seaboard of Southern India. All disputes were to

NATIVE BOATS ON THE GANGES IN BENGAL.

be brought before the governor in person and decided by him in open durbar, "because the English may have no wrong (behaving themselves as merchants ought to do)."

Next day the governor feasted the Englishmen and sent them contented away. They built a house of business at Hariharpur, on a channel half-way down the delta, and, as they fondly hoped, beyond the malaria of the swamps. Next month, June, 1633, Cartwright founded the factory of Balasor further up the coast, and near the present boundary between Orissa and Bengal. The Masulipatam Council gave loyal support, by sending on to him the *Swan* with her whole cargo, just arrived from England; and on July 22, 1633, she anchored off the Moghul customs-station of Harishpur. There she broke the silence of the swamps by firing three guns, but receiving no answer, sailed up the coast till she found Cartwright at Balasor.

Everything seemed to smile on the adventurers, and they projected outlying factories at Puri in the southern extremity, and at Pippli on the northern boundary of the Orissa seaboard. But their brief prosperity ended in disaster and death. The cargo of the *Swan*, chiefly broadcloth and lead, found no purchasers at Balasor, and lay for nearly a year unsold. The luscious fruits and cheap arak of Orissa formed temptations which the English sailors could not resist, and during the rainy season the deadly malaria of the swamps crept round their factory at Hariharpur in the mid-delta as round a beleaguered city.

Before the end of the year, five of our six factors in Orissa perished; the mortality among the sailors was terrible; and a second English ship sent thither had to make her way back to Madras with most of her crew stricken down by fever. It is difficult for us now to realize the miseries which the English, with their national habits of eating and drinking, suffered in the stifling forecastles and cabins of their ships, and in the

Kashmir Gate, Delhi.
From a Photograph.

mat-huts which formed their sole shelter on shore. Even a third of a century later, when they had learned in some measure to accommodate their dress and manner of living to the climate, two large English ships, after one year of the climate of Balasor, were unable to put out to sea "because most of their men were lost."

With their goods unsalable and factors and seamen dying around them, the survivors clung through the rainy season of 1633 to the footholds they had won on the Orissa coast. But two new scourges were added to their miseries. The Portuguese pirates from the Arakan and Chittagong seaboard, on the other side of the Bay of Bengal, swooped down on the river mouths; a Dutch fleet from the Madras coast and the Eastern Archipelago blockaded the roadsteads with pinnaces of ten to sixteen guns, strengthened by an occasional ship. Cartwright had to give up the idea of planting agencies at Pippli and Puri, the northern and southern extremities of Orissa; his central factory midway down the delta fell into decay, due in part to the silting up of the river; and soon all that remained to the English in Orissa was the unhealthy settlement at Balasor. The parent factory at Masulipatam had enough to do to keep its head above the all-engulfing wars between the inland king of Golconda and his half-subdued coast-rajas. The Company at home, in the grip of court cabals, looked on the Orissa settlements as a new and unprofitable burden which had been thrust upon it. In the words of Wilson's "Early Annals of Bengal," "No one cared about them; they were distant, unhealthy, dangerous." In 1641 the ship *Dyamond* was ordered thither to pay off their debts and bring away the factors.

But in the summer of 1642, after nine years' despairing struggle for existence, the tide began to turn. Francis Day, who had just founded Madras, visited Balasor and protested that it "is not to be totally left." After all, it lay within the Moghul Empire, whose settled order contrasted with the wild dynastic confusion further down the coast. The Madras Council shrank, however, from the risk, and referred the question home. Meanwhile the Company in London was exchanging the makeshift rule of Charles for the control of Parliament. In 1650 it resolved to follow the example of the Dutch and to found a settlement in Bengal itself. Yet the perils of the Hugli River, then unsurveyed and without lights or buoys, rendered it unsafe for large vessels. The Madras Council resolved therefore to make Balasor a port of trans-shipment, whence cargoes should be carried in native boats round to the Ganges delta, and so up its southwestern channel, the Hugli, to Hugli town, about a hundred miles from the sea.

There, on the bank of a deep pool formed by the current whirling round a bend of the river, the Portuguese had built a factory more than a century before. But having incurred, apparently, the displeasure of the Emperor Shah Jahan, while he was Prince Imperial, that sovereign soon after his accession resolved to root them out. On a petition to the throne "that some European idolaters, who had been allowed to establish factories in Hugli, had mounted their fort with cannon, and had grown insolent and oppressive," he took the city by storm in 1632; slew one thousand of the Portuguese (according to the native tradition), and carried off four thousand prisoners to his capital in Northern India, where the most beautiful of the girls were dis-

DIAMOND HARBOUR, AT THE MOUTH OF THE HUGLI RIVER.

tributed among the harems of his nobility. It is said that of sixty-four Portuguese ships and 257 smaller craft anchored opposite the town, only three small vessels escaped to sea.

A remnant lingered around their old monastery at Bandel, a mile higher up the Hugli, while the Dutch had a factory at Chinsurah, a little way down. The Dutch site was well chosen, for it marked the most inland point of the Ganges delta then accessible to sea-going ships. The ancient royal port of Bengal, on a creek which entered the river not far above Hugli town, had lately silted up, and the Moghul Government, after destroying the Portuguese settlement in 1632, made Hugli the imperial court for the Ganges provinces. Hugli remained the chief seat of the maritime trade of Bengal until the founding of Calcutta, half a century later.

The arrival of the English at Hugli in 1650 promised an accession of trade to the new imperial port, and an increased customs-revenue to the Moghul governor. They came as four peaceable merchants who had left their ship the *Lyoness* far off in the Balasor roadstead, and only asked leave to sell the goods brought up the river in small native boats. The letter of instructions drawn up for their guidance mingled religious admonition with shrewd commercial advice. "Principally and above all things," runs its opening paragraph, "you are to endeavour with the best of your might and power the advancement of the glory of God, which you will best do by walking holily, righteously, prudently, and Christianly in this present world," that so, "you may enjoy the quiet and peace of a good conscience toward God and man." In the next place they were to buy in the cheapest markets a cargo of Bengal sugars, silks, and "Peter" (saltpetre); to "enquire secretly" into the business methods of the Dutch; and above all to procure a license for trade which "may outstrip the Dutch in point of privilege and freedom." They carried with them an able Hindu, Narayan (or "Narrand") by name, who had been the "Company's broker" since our first settlement in Orissa in 1632, and who now repaid its confidence in the face of intrigues against him, by rendering good service to us in Bengal.

They also found a friend at the viceregal court then held at Raj Mahal, one of the shifting Ganges capitals, above the point where the mighty river splits

RAJ MAHAL ON THE GANGES.

up into its network of deltaic channels. Gabriel Boughton, doctor of the Company's ship *Hopewell*, had in 1645 been lent to a nobleman in the Imperial service, and was in 1650 Chirurgeon to the Moghul Viceroy of Bengal, Shah Shuja, who was a son of the reigning emperor, Shah Jahan. In or about the latter year Boughton obtained from his patron a license for free trade by the English in Bengal in return for three thousand rupees judiciously expended at the viceregal court. But as the document was lost three years later, by Mr. Waldegrave on a land journey to Madras, it remains doubtful whether the license confined our trade to the seaports or sanctioned it also in the interior. The Masulipatam factory rewarded Mr. Boughton with a gift "of gay apparel"—a dress of honour suitable to a high personage in attendance on the Viceregal Court —and from 1651 onward the English were established as traders alike on the seaboard and in the interior of Bengal. These trading posts were at Balasor, and perhaps at Pippli on the Orissa coast; at Hugli, Kasimbazar near Murshidabad, and one or two out-stations in the Ganges delta; and at Patna and subordinate agencies higher up the Ganges, in Behar.

It soon appeared that this advance northward exceeded the still feeble powers of the Company. The Bengal factories lay beyond effective control. Their staff, in spite of all pious instructions, plunged into irregularities which ended in two of them deserting the Company's service, in the death of a third ruined by debt, and in the return of a fourth to Madras with a story that he had lost the Company's papers. The good surgeon Boughton was also dead, and his widow, who had married again, was clamouring for a reward for his services. In 1656 - 1657 the Madras Council for the second time withdrew, or resolved to withdraw, their factories from the Bengal seaboard.

But once again we were saved from the counsels of despair. In October, 1657, Cromwell reorganized the Company on a broader basis. A commission to Bengal put down malpractices and re-established the trade. Hugli became the head agency in Bengal, with a control over the agencies at Balasor, on the Orissa coast, at Kasimbazar near Murshidabad, in the Gangetic delta, and at Patna on the higher Ganges in Behar, as well as a supervision over the out-stations or local houses for buying goods. Each factory had a chief, with three assistants or councillors, a regular subordination of authorities, and a code of rules for the conduct of life and of business. In the lowest grade of the new staff appears the name of a youth, Job Charnock—the future founder of Calcutta.

Bengal thus took its rank as one of the five important seats of the Company's trade, and was placed, together with Bantam and the Persian factories, under the control of Madras, itself subordinate to the presidency of Surat. The year 1658, the last of the Protector's life, saw the Company's affairs in the East remodelled upon a system of graduated dependence and control, under which its factories were to grow into settlements and finally into the British Indian Empire. The same year saw the deposition of the Indian sovereign, Shah Jahan, by his rebel son Aurangzib, and the commencement of the half-century of bigot rule under which the empire of the Moghuls slowly declined toward its fall.

APPENDIXES

APPENDIX I

THE COMPANY AND THE COMMONWEALTH

1649-1660

The preceding chapter ends with the various English settlements that grew finally into the British Indian Empire, as will be explained more fully in the next volume. As an appendix, however, I include here Sir William Hunter's valuable discussion of the relation of the Commonwealth under Cromwell to the affairs of India. A. V. W. J.

IN 1650 the East India Company, by command of the Council of State, effaced the king's arms still remaining on one of its ships. After the Restoration in 1660, it sought in like manner to hide the memorials of the Commonwealth, and the great charter of Cromwell disappeared from the India House. Its official historiographer, Bruce, the only annalist who has made a careful use of its archives, holds up the events of the intervening period as "an awful example" of a king and government "subverted by factions," "duped" by a "Usurper," and the "victim" of "guilty ambition." To the general historian those years appeared as a disastrous "scramble for the trade of India." Cromwell's own life was so full of great English interests, and so crowded by European events, that his biographers have found no leisure for his dealings with the East India Company.

Yet the manuscript records attest how decisive those dealings were. The East India trade ceases to be a pawn sacrificed to kings and queens in the game of royal marriages. It begins to stand out as a national interest, to be maintained by European treaties and enforced by a European war. In 1640, when the governor of the Company had rebuked "the generality" for their slack subscriptions notwithstanding the king's promises, they replied, according to the Ms. Court Book: "Until they shall see something *acted* by the King and State, men will not be persuaded to underwrite a new stock." They were now to come under a ruler chary of promise, but in action intrepid.

Cromwell found the Dutch triumphant in Europe and Asia, our Indian relations with the Portuguese still left to the haphazard of local conventions on the Bombay coast, and Amboyna unavenged. He enforced from Portugal an open trade for the English in the East; from Holland he wrung the long-denied redress for the torture and judicial slaughter of Englishmen in 1623, together with the restoration of the island then seized by the Dutch. Chief of all, he definitely imposed on the Company the principle of a permanent joint stock, on which it continued until its trade was thrown open in the nineteenth century. Under Cromwell's charter of 1657 was raised the first subscription destined not to be dissolved, but to grow into the permanent capital of the East India Company. The corporation passed, with little recognition of the change at the time, from its mediæval to its modern basis.

Born in 1599, the year when the London merchants met in Founders' Hall to project an East Indian voyage, Cromwell entered the House of Commons in 1628, the year of the Company's first appeal to Parliament. His charter of 1657 inaugurated the three cyclic dates of Great Britain in the East. It was fitly commemorated by the Battle of Plassey in 1757, and by the reconquest of India after the Sepoy Revolt, exactly one hundred years later.

But before his strong hand could make its weight felt, a period intervened when there was no king in Israel. From the Battle of Edgehill, in October, 1642, to the last scene outside Whitehall in January, 1649, Charles, whatever may have been his faults, cannot be held accountable for the distresses of the East India Company. One Parliament, with the king, a majority of the Lords, and a minority of the Commons, sat at Oxford. Another Parliament, with a majority of the Commons and a minority of the Lords, sat at Westminster. It was with this London Parliament that the Company had to reckon. The Houses at Westminster could levy contributions in the capital, they collected the customs, and controlled the shipping in the Thames. In 1643 they put a curb on the Royalist members of the Company by demanding a forced loan of its ordnance, "for the fortifying of the bulwarks, now in preparation for the security of the City." On its refusal, the Commons declared they would grant an order to the Committee of Fortifications to take them. So the cannon had to be given up, and the next year the Company petitioned for payment or their return.

The London Parliament was, in truth, in no mood to tolerate a king's faction within the liberties of the City. In 1643 it cashiered the Company's governor, sequestrated moneys due to Royalists at the India House, and forbade any dividends to be paid until the directors had had an interview with a committee of the Lords and Commons. Later in the year, the Parliamentary Government demanded a loan of £10,000, and the Company was glad to get off for half that sum. By 1644 the Royalist party in the Company was cowed, and the chief officers of its ships had taken the Solemn League and Covenant.

This coercion cost the Company dear. It had lately opened houses in Italy to dispose of its Indian goods, almost unsalable amid the troubles at home, and in 1645 one of its Royalist members, Sir Peter Rychaut, revenged his sequestrations in England by seizing three hundred bags of its pepper in Venice. Its captains, when clear of the Thames, were sometimes difficult to control. Captain Mucknell of the ship *John*, for example, carried his ship into Bristol and delivered it to the king's general. He then sallied forth with three armed vessels to waylay other Indiamen, and the Company was advised to despatch two nimble pinnaces to scout among the Western Islands or Azores and warn its homeward-bound vessels of their danger.

Amid this confusion, the Company still tried to

A STREET SCENE IN BOMBAY.

make a show of trade. With no hope from the king, by whose charter it existed, and in little favour with Parliament, it found its position almost as isolated as that of its servants in India. Like them, it evoked from the sense of desertion a resolve to rely upon itself. It entered, as we shall see, into direct negotiations with the Portuguese ambassador in London, and it almost succeeded in coming to an arrangement with the Dutch. It also began to strike out new trade methods. In 1640, with the help of royal promises, it had tried to raise fresh capital under the name of the Fourth Joint Stock. But the public had lost confidence, and with the shares selling as low as sixty per cent., the money could not be obtained.

Yet individual expeditions, if conducted without a dead outlay on factories, forts, and a permanent staff in India, yielded large profits. Laying aside for the time the project of a Fourth Joint Stock, some of its members subscribed in 1641 for a Particular Voyage, which should engage no servants in the East, but pay a commission to the Third Joint Stock for selling its goods and collecting a return cargo. Others began to take heart and got together a small nucleus for the Fourth Joint Stock. This double organization of individual voyages and a general stock led to grave difficulties, as it tried to combine the early plan of Separate Voyages with the Joint Stocks, or series of voyages, which had superseded them. Yet it enabled the Company to struggle through the civil wars without altogether losing its continuity of trade.

That fate was narrowly averted. In 1647, when the House of Lords rejected the "Ordinance for the Trade," which the Commons had passed as a Parliamentary charter for the Company, the governor called together the shareholders. He explained to them that, while they had lost the privileges, they remained subject to the responsibilities of the royal grant. "Every man had liberty to go to India," but the Indian princes held the Company "liable for what depredations" any Englishman might there commit. In this way they had already lost £100,000, besides another £100,000 from Courten's trading. Courten's Association, having reached the end of its resources, was carrying on business with counterfeit coin, pagodas, and reals, which it manufactured on a great scale at Madagascar, and so brought the English name into disgrace throughout the East. The Indian princes made the Company responsible for this and similar offences. The governor advised the brethren, therefore, "to draw home their factors and estate," and the Company decided to wind up the Fourth Joint Stock. "In regard to the troubles of the times," they abandoned the idea of forming a new Joint Stock, but in order that the trade might not be wholly lost, they decided to find money for another voyage.

Cromwell viewed the India trade from a national standpoint, and regarded the Company as one of several alternative methods for conducting it. When a protracted inquiry convinced him that it was the method best suited to the times, he strongly supported it. But throughout he had the interest not of the Company, but of the nation, in mind. As he set himself, while still a cavalry colonel, to form an army of victory at home, so he resolved, as head of the Commonwealth, to create a marine which should give England predominance abroad. The Navigation Act of 1651 served as his New Model for winning the supremacy of the seas. The East India Company, its charters, and its rivals, were merely instruments for carrying out this great design.

Yet if Cromwell long stood aloof from the Company in its domestic distresses, he lost no time in dealing with its foreign enemies. In 1650 it petitioned "the Supreme Authority of this Nation, the High Court of the Parliament of England," for help against Holland. After a list of Dutch injuries, involving an alleged loss of two millions sterling during the past twenty years, it declared that it had repeatedly laid its wrongs before the king and Council, and had prayed in vain "that satisfaction should be demanded from the States-General." Parliament received the petition with favour, and on the same day voted that it be referred for consideration by the Council of State. But Cromwell had Scotland on his hands, and he intended, if a Dutch war must come, to wage it on wider issues. So next year, 1651, the Company twice brought its Dutch grievances before the Council of State, and again in January, 1652. Cromwell was now ready, and the wrongs of the East India Company furnished one of the causes of the war with Holland declared in the following summer. Next year the Company supplied saltpetre for the navy, and offered to equip a fleet of its own, which, with the aid of a few ships to be lent by the government, would turn the Dutch flank by carrying the war into the Indian seas. The proposal was not accepted, but compensation to the East India Company figured largely among the final spoils of victory. In 1653 a Dutch fleet threatened our factory at Surat. The Moghul government, however, did not allow private wars between Europeans within its dominions, so the Hollanders sailed to the Persian Gulf, where they captured three English ships. The Company's trade at Bantam was also suspended during the war.

A NATIVE BOAT OF THE PERSIAN GULF.

By the treaty of 1654, which restored peace, Holland pledged herself "that justice should be done upon those who were partakers or accomplices in the massacre of the English at Amboyna, as the Republic of England is pleased to term that fact," and sent commissioners to London to settle all money claims. By this time the torturers and the tortured had alike passed away; it only remained to offer some solatium to the heirs of the victims and to compensate the Company for its losses. Twelve years previously the Company, hopeless of action by the king, was willing to compound privately with the Dutch for a payment of

£50,000, and the negotiations had broken down only as the Dutch demanded the relinquishment of its rights in the island of Pularoon. It now produced a swollen bill of two and one-half millions sterling for Dutch injuries perpetrated from 1611 to 1652. The Dutch gravely replied by counter-claims amounting to nearly three millions.

But the Protector was not to be trifled with, and had resolved that any questions left open at the end of three months should be referred for arbitration to the Protestant Swiss Cantons. So the commissioners made short work of the huge totals, and, striking a balance, declared that the Dutch Company must pay £85,000 to the London Company, besides £3615 to the heirs or executors of the Amboyna victims, and must restore Pularoon to the English. The sum thus awarded to the London Company was more than half as much again as that for which it would, in its despondency, have settled privately with the Dutch in 1642. Oliver sternly let it know, however, that it held Pularoon only in trust, and must "plant and manage the island so that it may not be lost to the nation."

In the same summer of 1654, Cromwell put an end for ever to the exclusive claims of Portugal in the East—claims based on the Papal Bull of 1493, but embodied during a century and a half in the public law of Europe. With regard to this matter also the Company had tried to accomplish by private negotiation what royal diplomacy had failed to effect. The commercial convention between its president at Surat and the Goa viceroy in 1635 seemed to open the door to an international settlement of the Indies. When the instrument reached England, the Company applied to King Charles and to his minister at Madrid with this end in view, as usual without practical result. After the separation of the crowns of Spain and Portugal in 1640, our Surat president again entered into negotiations on his own account with the Goa viceroy, and obtained from him letters to the Portuguese ambassador in London. The directors in England also addressed his Excellency. But the Portuguese ambassador distrusted their amateur diplomacy and would grant no settled peace in the Indies; indeed, only a further truce for two years. In 1642 Charles I, while arranging for freedom of trade between England and Portugal, agreed that their relations in India should remain for three years more on the basis of the local Surat-Goa Convention.

Cromwell had no liking for such private negotiations. Resenting the shelter given by Portugal to Prince Rupert's fleet, he prepared the way for peace by Blake's cannon, and three months after the Dutch submission he extorted a final settlement from Portugal. His Portuguese treaty of July, 1654, placed on an international basis the right of English ships to trade to any Portuguese possession in the East Indies.

In all this Cromwell made no pretence of special favour to the Company. To him the India trade was one of the great English interests to be subserved by the treaties which followed European wars. Yet as the Company was a chief gainer from the national successes, he thought it should contribute to their cost. In 1649 the commissioners of the navy constrained it to lend £4000; in July, 1655, Cromwell borrowed from it £50,000; and in October of the same year another £10,000 to pay Blake's seamen. These loans were strictly applied to public purposes and faithfully repaid.

But Cromwell expected from the Company not money alone. In 1652 the Council demanded from it, without success, two ships of war "for Defence of the Right and Honour of this Nation." To secure Pularoon the Company was called, in 1656, to provide £30,000 for fortifications, guard-pinnaces, and cannon, together with a garrison of eighty Englishmen and over two hundred native soldiers. As the Dutch rooted up the spice-trees before they even pretended to deliver over the island, no speedy return could be expected. Indeed, the money had to be levied by a contribution from the shareholders of twenty per cent. on their original ventures. When, therefore, the Protector started, also in 1656, his project of a volunteer fleet, the Company found itself compelled to hold aloof. He ordered it to send representatives to arrange with other trading bodies and himself for the equipment of thirty-nine men-of-war as convoys. The wearied directors replied that the existing dues already amounted to ten per cent., and that they could not possibly pay more.

By this time Cromwell had inquired into the affairs of the Company and knew that it could not bear further burdens. But while considerate to its distresses, he brooked no private diplomacy such as the Company had carried on during the late reign with the Dutch and Portuguese. In the moment of granting his charter of 1657, the Protector called it sharply to task for attempting to negotiate on its own account with Holland. The directors had sought redress from the Dutch ambassador in London for a fresh infringement of their rights in the East. His Excellency, like most foreign representatives under Cromwell's rule, proved gracious. But the Protector intimated his displeasure at the Company's approaching a foreign minister without his knowledge, and commanded it to submit all grievances to himself.

While Cromwell thus both strengthened and controlled the Company in regard to its foreign enemies, he intervened with reluctance between it and domestic rivals. For several years after the death of King Charles the task of constructing a government in England, and of defending it by arms, left him no leisure for trade wrangles. The Council of State, which meanwhile carried on the civil administration, found itself besieged by three sets of applicants for the Eastern traffic. Foremost among them was the Company, founding its monopoly on a royal charter, but on a royal charter so tampered with by royalty itself as to have lost much of its value. Next came Courten's Association, which also based its claims on a royal grant. In the background the great merchants of London and Bristol, belonging to neither of these societies, clamoured for an open trade in the joint interests of themselves and the nation. We have seen that the attempt in 1647 to embody the Company's charter into an Act of Parliament failed; the Ordinance for the Trade, although it passed through the Commons, was rejected by the House of Lords. After the king's death in 1649,

SHOP OF A MERCHANT OF THE VAISYA CASTE.

therefore, the Council of State had to face the whole question anew.

It did so in no revolutionary spirit. Without going into constitutional questions as to how far a trade-charter from King James held good under the Commonwealth, it took up the matter as it was left by the abortive action of Parliament in 1647. It counselled the Company to come to terms with Courten's Association, and it refused to interfere until they themselves arrived at a settlement. Both the rivals had reached the brink of ruin. Courten's Association, or the Assada Merchants as they were now called from their plantation on Assada Isle at Madagascar, were almost bankrupt. We have seen them reduced to carrying on their trade by a manufacture of counterfeit coin, and they had offered to surrender their factories on the Indian coast to the Company's president at Surat, having offered him Karwar in 1645 - 1646 and Rajapur in 1649. In 1651, they made a similar offer of their Madagascar settlement, Assada itself. The East India Company, on its part, found it impossible either to raise a new Joint Stock or to go on with its old capital, and had to fall back on another "Particular Voyage." Indeed, in 1649, it passed a resolution of despair not to send out any more ships, either upon the Joint Stock or Separate Voyage system after April of that year.

Yet only after long strife could the disputants come to terms. In 1649 they agreed that the two societies should work together as regards the general Indian trade; that Courten's Association should retain its Assada factory at Madagascar and have liberty to traffic thence to all Asiatic and African countries; while the port to port trade in India should be reserved to the Company. The business in gold and ivory on the coast of Guinea should be open to both.

Their compact was embodied in a petition to Parliament, and on January 31, 1650, the House of Commons resolved: "That the trade to the East Indies should be carried on by one Company, and with one Joint Stock, and the management thereof to be under such regulations as the Parliament shall think fit, and that the East India Company should proceed upon the articles of agreement made between them and the Assada Merchants on November 21, 1649, until further orders from the Parliament." This coalition of the rival bodies under a Parliamentary sanction formed the basis on which the India trade continued until Cromwell's charter toward the close of the Commonwealth.

At first all was concord. The day after the Parliamentary vote, the two associations proposed to form a "United Joint Stock," which should take over the factories in India, and continue to trade for three years. But in vain the Company's beadle went round to the freemen with the subscription book. Money would not come in, and extraordinary methods were employed to raise capital. The Company sent letters to thirteen of the port-towns of England inviting them to join; and blank subscription books, with a preamble setting forth the nature of the adventure, were humbly laid before the Parliament and Council of State. The members of these honourable bodies would not venture a penny; and even the offer of the freedom of the Company, once so valued, failed to tempt the general public. The thirteen port-towns were equally unresponsive. The governor had to announce that replies had been received from only Bristol and Exeter; and there seemed no likelihood of money being obtained from that source. The Assada Merchants having barely the funds to carry on their own business, could furnish but little to the new Joint Stock. With such sums as its own exhausted members were able to subscribe, the Company struggled on.

How hard was the struggle abundantly appears in the records. The continued existence of the Company depended not on the continuity of its trade or on its sending out a yearly succession of ships. As long as it elected in each July a governor and the other officers named in the charter of James I it preserved its existence as a body corporate in the eye of the law. In July, 1651, the question arose whether it was worth while to keep up this formality. The General Court decided, however, to proceed with the election of officers, although "hereafter there will be little use of any governor, in regard they are to set no ships out, nor much other business but to pay their debts."

The fact is that the union of the Company and the Assada Merchants failed to cope with the situation. For outside these societies a body of capitalists had grown up who protested against the monopoly of the India trade as a relic of the royal prerogative no longer suited to the times. They claimed that the Eastern traffic should either be organized on the Regulated system, under which each member of a trade guild or association might traffic on his own account, as in the Turkey Company, or that it should be thrown open to the nation. This feeling had at first expressed itself in a demand for increased state protection of foreign trade. "It is not our conquests, but our commerce," runs a powerful appeal by Lewes Roberts in 1641, just after the meeting of the Long Parliament, "it is not

A ROAD SCENE IN INDIA IN THE BOMBAY PRESIDENCY.

our swords but our sayls, that first spred the English name in Barbary, and thence came (*sic*) into Turkey, Armenia, Moscovia, Arabia, Persia, India, China, and indeed over and about the world. It is the traffic of their merchants and the boundless desires of that nation to eternize the English honour and name, that hath enduced them to saile and seek into all the corners of the earth."

Under the Commonwealth the desire for an open trade to India gained strength. The Navigation Act of 1651 gave it a decisive impulse. Next year—the very year after the Company had declared that thenceforth "there will be little use of any governor, in regard they are to set no ships out"—a new voice rang aloud to the nation: "That with all possible conveniency we enlarge our Forraign Plantations, and get further footing in Barbarie, East and West Indies." Forasmuch as "a little spot of ground, as England is, with its Dominions, if it do not enlarge them," will strive in vain against the growing trade of Holland and the other European powers. Men of rank once again joined with men of the City in ventures beyond the seas. Indeed in 1649 the Company had complained that the name of Lord General Fairfax stood first in the draft of a patent for the Assada Merchants which it was intended to submit to Parliament.

The outside capitalists hoped that after the three years for which the United Joint Stock of 1650 was formed, a broader basis might be adopted. But on the expiration of that period in the summer of 1653 the Company found itself too weak to attempt any new departure, and the existing arrangement continued, although no ships could be sent out. Forthwith it appeared that the outsiders had strong supporters within the Company itself. The standard of revolt was raised at a court meeting in the following December, when one of the generality proposed that individual members should, as under the Regulated system, be allowed to trade on their own account. The traffic was passing into the hands of interlopers, and if the Company could not send forth ships itself, why should it preclude its members from doing so?

The governing body found it difficult to answer this argument, and temporized by allowing private members to trade to India on a payment to the Company for the privilege. But the concession amounted to a change from the Joint Stock to the Regulated system, in opposition to the terms of the late Parliamentary settlement of 1650. So in March, 1654, the governing body took a firmer stand. They decided that "it is not in the power of this Court to give liberty to any private persons to trade to India; but if any do it, it is at their own peril. And thereupon the votes of Parliament were read, concerning the carrying on of the trade in a Joint Stock."

Issue was thus definitely joined between the two great parties which have always divided mercantile opinion in England with regard to the Indian trade. Under the first Stuarts the conflict was waged between the Company and individuals or associations licensed, in infringement of the Company's charter, by the king. Under the Commonwealth it widened into a struggle between the conservative section of the Company and a forward party within itself, but allied to the outside capitalists who claimed an open trade to India. Under the Restoration it became a war of law-suits between the Company and the independent mercantile community at large; a war ended only by the great Parliamentary amalgamation after the Revolution. That settlement lasted down to the 19th century, when even its broad basis was found too narrow for the expansive forces of British commerce, and the Act of 1813 threw open the India trade to the nation. The records of the East India Company form a concentrated history of the English hatred of monopoly; of the Company's efforts to maintain exclusive privileges by from time to time widening its doors, as long as the country believed exclusive privileges necessary for the India trade; and of their abolition as soon as the country thought them no longer required.

Meanwhile the Parliamentary settlement of 1650, in subjecting the trade to further regulation by the Commons, provided for such difficulties as arose under the Commonwealth. The Council of State recognized the claims of the outside merchants by a cautious yet liberal issue of licenses for private trade to India. Cromwell's name begins to appear in connection with these grants, not only to individuals, but also to the Merchant Adventurers, and it seemed to onlookers both at home and abroad that the Company was doomed. Nine months after it had taken up its rigid attitude against private trading by its own members in 1654, the Amsterdam burghers received "advice that the Lord Protector will dissolve the East India Company at London, and declare the navigation and commerce to the Indies to be free and open." The mere rumour of the nationalizing of England's Eastern trade sent a thrill of apprehension through Holland.

Meanwhile the expansive forces within the Company burst forth beyond control. In the autumn of 1654 the section of its freemen in favour of private enterprise had petitioned the Council of State that the East India trade be still carried on by a company, but with liberty for the members individually to trade with their own

DACCA, NEAR CALCUTTA, IN BENGAL.

capital and ships in such way as they might deem most to their advantage. The Company urged in reply that the experience of forty years proved that the India trade could be conducted only by an association strongly bound together by a series of Joint Stocks, and that the plan of Separate Voyages had been given up after a full trial; that the Company had now factories beneath fourteen native sovereigns, together with a costly equipment necessary for the protection of so distant a trade; and that, under its engagements with the Indian powers, it was held responsible by them for depredations or misconduct of all Englishmen in the East. It accordingly prayed the Protector to grant it a new and wider charter, to the exclusion of private trade.

In 1654, therefore, Cromwell found himself called on to decide between the three sets of applicants: the outside capitalists who desired that the commerce with India should be thrown open to the nation; the governing body of the Company who asked for wider privileges upon the basis of a series of exclusive Joint Stocks; and the section of its members who desired that the Company should be transferred from the Joint Stock to the Regulated system. His clear eye saw that if the India trade were to be thrown open to the nation, it must be protected by the national arms. He realized that neither the navy nor the land forces of the Commonwealth was adapted for such a task. He accordingly eased the situation by granting trade licenses to individual outsiders, and referred the main question as to the future constitution of the Company to the Council of State.

The Council soon found itself plunged in a quagmire of irreconcilable claims. A question even arose as to which of the several sets of adventurers really represented the Company. When the Dutch compensation of £85,000 came to be distributed, the survivors or heirs of the Third Joint Stock, of the Fourth Joint Stock, and of the United Joint Stock asserted their several rights to it. The Council could find a way out of its bewilderment only by referring their titles to arbitration, and meanwhile, in 1655, lodged the money with trustees. Cromwell hastened a decision by borrowing £50,000 of the compensation fund for the State.

If such a confusion of claims existed within the Company itself, the conflict on the wider issue as to the future management of the India trade may be imagined. During two years the Council of State laboured for a settlement in vain. The governing body of the Company lost hope, and its Court of Committees resolved in 1656 to sell its "privileges and houses in India . . . to some Englishmen," at a valuation of £14,000, retaining, however, a share with the purchasers in the future trade. But the General Court overruled this decision, and on October 20, 1656, sent up one more petition to Cromwell.

On the very same day the Protector, under his own hand, referred the petition to the Council of State, and took care that that body now appointed a committee which should carry his own vigorous resolve into its task. While great names and high office gave weight to its deliberations, the actual work was entrusted to a man in whom he placed complete confidence. Colonel Philip Jones, after suffering much and fighting hard on behalf of the Parliament, became a leading member of the Council of State and filled important offices under the Commonwealth. In the previous year, 1655, Oliver had selected him as sole arbiter in a delicate question between England and Portugal; in 1657 he was one of the committee appointed to offer to Cromwell the crown: and as controller of the household he superintended the Protector's funeral in 1658. It was on this tried friend that Oliver chiefly leant for advice "in what manner the East India trade might be best managed for the public good and its own encouragement." Colonel Jones was specially charged "to take care thereof."

His prompt action indicates that Cromwell had already made up his mind on the evidence before him. In six weeks Colonel Jones and his colleagues accomplished what the Council of State had failed to do during two years—they arrived at a settlement for the India trade. The committee's report was signed by only three members: one of whom, Colonel William Sydenham, had lately stood forth in Parliament as Cromwell's mouthpiece for religious toleration; another, Colonel Philip Jones, already mentioned, was the controller of his household; while the third, Sir Charles Wolseley, was his most intimate confidant. They were of the opinion that the India trade should be carried on by one company on the basis of a United Joint Stock, yet they sent the matter back to the Council of State as being too high for them to decide. The Council of State again procrastinated, but under severe pressure, as we shall see, adopted the report, and referred it for final orders to the Protector.

To the decision of this great issue Cromwell brought a slow but effective training. He had been a member of the Commission of Trade and Plantations in 1643, at the moment when the commercial prerogatives of the Crown passed in reality from the king to the Parliament. Years of war and internal struggle followed. But as soon as Cromwell firmly established the Commonwealth, his mercantile policy took a definite shape. The Navigation Act of 1651 laid the foundation of England's mercantile ascendency, and formed a chief cause of the Dutch war in the following year. Even before Cromwell granted peace to Holland, he seems to have resolved on a similar assertion of power over the Catholic nations. From Portugal he enforced the English liberty of trade in the East Indies; and his West Indian expedition against Spain, in 1654-1655, had its origin in mercantile not less than in political reasons. Not only in European waters, but throughout all the ocean-world from Malabar to Hispaniola, Oliver determined to make England supreme. In 1655 the chief economic writer of the time presented to the Protector his mature work, and in the same year Cromwell appointed the Committee of Trade—"a great concernment of the Commonwealth," says Carlyle, "'which his Highness is eagerly set upon.'"

Cromwell perceived that, as the time had not yet come for an open trade to India, to be supported by a national fleet in Asiatic seas, the real question lay between a Regulated Company, the members of which might trade on their individual account, and a Joint Stock Company. The analogy of the Turkey Company, confidently relied on by the advocates of the Regulated system, did not bear scrutiny. For the dealings of the Turkey Company were chiefly with the Mediterranean powers—Venetians, Spaniards, Barbary Corsairs, and

Turks—within the reach of English diplomacy and of English reprisals. When the Doge laid prohibitive customs on our Levant trade, Elizabeth forbade the Venetian import into England of the raisins of Corinth and the wines of Candia, until the Adriatic Republic should take off its imposts. Cromwell had just given sharp proof to Spain and the Barbary Corsairs that they were both within range of his guns. As regards Turkey, the very year after James I granted a charter in perpetuity to the merchants of England in the Levant, it was found necessary to appoint an English envoy to the Grand Seignior, and to establish consuls within his dominions. International relations sprang up and eventually developed into a system of consular jurisdiction for the protection of English subjects in the eastern Mediterranean. It is said that in 1685 the only English diplomatic agent with the title of ambassador resided at Constantinople, and was paid in part by the Turkey Company. But no statesman believed, in 1657, that the Moghul Empire could be called to a reckoning by English diplomacy or arms, or that the Commonwealth should maintain a permanent embassy at Agra, and a cordon of consuls around the Indian coast. The plea for a Regulated East India Company from the analogy of the Regulated Turkey Company proved to be no argument at all.

The real evidence which confronted Cromwell lay in the history of the East India Company itself. Even before Elizabeth granted her charter, its founders had declared in 1599 " that the trade of the Indias being so far remote from hence cannot be traded but in a joint and united stock." Yet the actual charters of Elizabeth and James contained no reference to the sub-

DOMES OF A MOSQUE OF THE MOGHUL PERIOD.

ject, nor was a continuous joint stock ever raised. The truth is that the term "Joint Stock" had to the founders in 1599 a very different meaning from that connoted by its modern development, the "Joint Stock Company." It signified only a subscription for a joint voyage, whose accounts were to be wound up and the capital repaid when the ships came home. The East India Company was a body corporate with an exclusive grant of the India trade from the Crown, and it conducted its business by forming successive groups among its own members for raising joint stock subscriptions for successive and distinct ventures.

At first, indeed, it differed but slightly from the Turkey and other Regulated Companies of mediæval commerce, except that the right of separate trading passed from the individual freemen to successive groups of freemen—a statement which must be taken subject to the full explanation given in the chapter on the Constitution of the Company in the preceding volume. On this basis the Company equipped its first nine voyages. When the system of Separate Voyages proved too weak to cope with its Portuguese and Dutch rivals in the East, it raised a series of Joint Stock subscriptions, each of which supplied the capital for a distinct series of voyages. But the Joint Stock subscription was designed only for a limited number of years, at the end of which it was to be wound up—in short, the original system of Separate Voyages gave place to a system of separate series of voyages. Every new Joint Stock was intended to take over at a valuation the factories of its predecessor in India. In this rudimentary form of Joint Stock the group of members took the place of the individual freeman, as the group of voyages took the place of the individual venture, in a "Regulated" association like the Turkey Company.

Amid the troubles of the Civil War the system of separate series or groups of voyages broke down. But although money could not be raised for a series of voyages, there were, as we have seen, men both inside and outside the Company ready to stake a sufficient sum for a single voyage, if freed from the burden of the capital sunk in India. Such attempts to combine the original system of Separate Voyages with that of Joint Stock series of voyages led to a demand for the individual freedom of each member of the Company to trade on his own account—in short, for a reversion from the successive and distinct series of Joint Stocks back to the old Regulated system. The resistance of the governing body of the Company to this demand produced the petitions and counter-petitions on which the Council of State had so long been unable to decide.

Colonel Jones's report was presented to the Council of State on December 18, 1656. That body renewed its old hesitations, and the Company, in anger and despair, resolved on January 14, 1657, that unless a decision were received within a month, it would make sale of its factories, rights, and customs in India "to any natives of this commonwealth to and for their own proper use." There was now no mention of its taking a share with the purchasers, and it evidently contemplated a complete withdrawal from the trade. It ordered bills of sale to be hung up in the London Exchange. The Council of State, thus galvanized into action, summoned the Company and the rival merchant adventurers for a final hearing, and advised the Protector "that the trade of India be managed by a United Joint Stock exclusive of all others." Forthwith, on February 10, 1657, Cromwell directed that a committee should sit to draw up a charter, which on October 19th passed the Broad Seal of England.

After the Restoration the Company hastened to purge itself of complicity with the Commonwealth, and the document disappeared. A diligent inquiry now leaves no hope that a copy survives in England, Holland, or the East. But although the charter has perished, I have been able, from contemporary documents, to piece together its main provisions. It ratified the charter of James I with slight modifications, and gave additional privileges. As new coast towns had sprung into vigour, the original three ports (London, Dartmouth, and Plymouth), from which bullion might be exported, were to be increased to seven. On the other hand, the clauses granting the powers of Law Martial and immunity from customs, tonnage, and poundage, and certain other privileges, were to be omitted, and left to be dealt with by special orders from the Protector, who should also have the right to recall the charter if he saw cause. Cromwell's charter, in fact, combined the substance of the Royal Charter of 1609 with the more continuous government-control provided by the Parliamentary grant of 1650. The Protector promised that his settlement should in the next session be confirmed by Act of Parliament.

Cromwell died the following year before a Parliamentary sanction could be obtained, and his charter

Smaller Gopura in West Court, Madura.
From a Photograph.

formed the last word of the Commonwealth on the three sets of proposals which had so long divided English merchants: namely, for an open commerce to India, for a Regulated Company, and for a Joint Stock Company. He reconstituted the India trade on the basis of "One Joint Stock." The words "Joint Stock" do not occur in the charters of Elizabeth or James I, nor, indeed, in any royal charter until that of 1686. The Company's so called "Joint Stocks" had been merely successive subscriptions for separate sets of voyages; each set being a distinct and several adventure to be wound up at the end of a fixed number of years. The idea of a united joint stock, which emerged in the Parliamentary settlement of 1650, developed under Cromwell's charter of 1657 into a united and continuous joint stock.

The change was wrought not by Cromwell alone, but by Cromwell representing the spirit of the times. If the Protector prescribed unity, the Company interpreted unity to imply also continuity and permanence. The very day that the charter passed the Broad Seal, a General Court held at the India House laid down the conditions under which it should be carried out. These conditions, as finally settled, threw open the freedom of the Company to the public for the nominal sum of £5. They admitted not only the members of the various groups who had made up the old East India and Assada Companies, together with their servants and apprentices, but also all those Merchant Adventurers and private traders in India who might be willing to throw their possessions, at a fair valuation, into the common stock.

That stock was not to be dissolved after the expiration of a few years, as had always been provided in

A CROWD IN A BUSY INDIAN EMPORIUM.

former subscriptions. An appraisement of the Company's property was to be made at the end of seven years, and thereafter at the end of every three years, so that any shareholder who wished to retire might do so, and receive the current value of his original subscription. But the Joint Stock was to continue as the common capital of the Company, and the money drawn out by retiring members was to be made good by "any other persons" who chose to join the Company. As a matter of fact, these triennial appraisements resolved themselves into periodical statements of assets by which the members and the public might regulate their dealings in the stock.

Cromwell thus laid the groundwork of the modern constitution of the East India Company. Under the regulations based on his charter, it cast its mediæval skin, shook off the traditions of the Regulated system, and grew into one united, continuous, and permanent Joint Stock Corporation in the full sense of the words.

These new conditions of unity and permanence drew forth a large capital of £739,782—of which only one-half was called up. The minimum subscription was fixed at £100; a contributor had a vote for each £500 of his holding; and £1000 qualified for election to the committee. Small adventurers might club together to make up £500, and appoint one of their number to vote for them. The actual management of the Company was vested, as under the royal charters, in a governor, deputy-governor, treasurer, and a committee of twenty-four. With the ample funds at its disposal, the new association bought up the factories, forts, customs, and privileges of the old Company in the East, including the island of Pularoon, for £20,000; arranged for taking over the properties of individual adventurers in

India at a valuation; and resolved to unite the Guinea traffic in gold and elephant tusks with the India trade.

While thus amalgamating the various conflicting interests into one permanent Joint Stock, the new Company provided ample safeguards for its own monopoly. Outside traders continued subject to the same penalties as those laid down by King James's charter—the confiscation of their ship and cargo. Members inside the Company, who might still hanker after the Regulated system and be tempted to trade on their own account, were to forfeit their whole stock or holding to the rest of the shareholders. Fair consideration was extended to all actually engaged, under whatever show of title, in Indian ventures in the past; but there was to be no mercy for private traders, whether inside the Company or outside it, in the future.

Although resolved on a firm control of its individual members, the Company made provision for a steady flow of new men from the generality to its governing body. That body consisted, as I have said, of a governor, deputy-governor, and committee of twenty-four. But eight members of the committee were to retire in rotation each July, and no governor or deputy-governor was to serve for more than two successive years. The freemen were also to be relieved of the old inconvenience of having to receive their individual shares of the profits in pepper, calicoes, or other Indian commodities, and all dividends were henceforth to be paid in cash. In the East the New Company received in return for its £20,000 the Old Company's factories at Surat, with dependencies on the Bombay coast; at Fort St. George, with dependencies on the Madras coast and in the Bay of Bengal; at Bantam, with dependencies at Jambi, Macassar, and Pularoon; and at Gombroon on the Persian Gulf.

The small price paid for these acquisitions is explained by the circumstances of the times. On the Persian Gulf the agents of the Old Company had struggled on amid oppressions and exactions, not because they hoped to do any trade, but merely on the chance of reasserting, at some future day, the English right to half the customs of Gombroon under the treaty of 1622. Bantam seemed again to be passing under the power of the Dutch, English ships were intercepted in the narrow seas, and the port was about to suffer a regular blockade. Nor did the political state of India itself warrant any large price for English possessions on that continent.

The military convulsions, amid which Aurangzib seized the throne, rudely interrupted the order that the Moghul Empire had during a century imposed. Surat castle was seized and the town pillaged on behalf of one of the claimants; and the distracted president complained "that it was equally dangerous to solicit, or to accept of, protection, it being impossible to foresee who might ultimately be the Moghul." In Southern India, the first great act of Maratha hostility to the Moghuls took place in May, 1657. On the east coast, the Madras Council in despair resolved for the second time to withdraw the factories from Bengal. Their own existence was threatened by the war between the Golkonda king and his dependents, and by the still more dreaded approach of the Maratha hordes.

Thus in the very year that Cromwell's charter recon-

THE EMPEROR AURANGZIB AND HIS COURT.

stituted the Company on its permanent basis at home, the English in the Eastern seas, from the Persian Gulf to the island of Java, stood face to face with ruin. In India itself, the firm Moghul rule, under whose shelter our settlements on the continent had grown up, was for the first time assailed by that combination of Moslem disunion and Hindu confederate force which, during the next fifty years, broke up the empire.

The new Company went courageously to work. It decided that Surat, then in the grip of civil war, should be its sole presidency in India, and that the factories at Madras, Bengal, Bantam, and the Persian Gulf should be distinct agencies subordinate thereto. All these settlements were destitute alike of money and men. On the Persian Gulf the bare subsistence of the factory consumed the customs of Gombroon and the whole profits of the trade. The late Company had ordered the establishment at Madras to be reduced to two factors with a guard of ten soldiers, and to a single factor at Masulipatam. From every English settlement in the East came the same story of decay. The new Company at once resolved to send out such a staff as never had sailed to India.

In January, 1658, it selected seventeen of the late Company's most likely stations in the East, from China to the Persian Gulf, and appointed to them ninety-one factors and assistants, well supplied with goods and bullion for the re-establishment of the trade. When an adventurer, under plea of a license from the Commonwealth, shipped mortars and shells for one of the rival claimants to the Moghul throne, the Company firmly remonstrated with Cromwell, and at the same time despatched a consignment to undersell the interloper. On the west coast of Africa it bought up Fort Comantine, together with the charter, rights, and trade of the Guinea Company, for the modest sum of £1300. In the mid-ocean it resolved to fortify St. Helena, as a half-way house for the Indian fleets. In the Far East it projected a place of strength at Pularoon, and applied to Richard Cromwell for letters to the emperors of China and Japan. From the charter of 1657 the Company drew a new life, whose pulsations reached its farthest factories in Asia. Against European aggressors it boldly claimed the aid of the Commonwealth. More than once it invoked Cromwell's intervention against Holland; and the Company's last transaction with the Protector was still another petition against the Dutch. Three weeks later the strong ruler was dead, and about to be laid with royal pomp in Westminster Abbey.

After the Restoration men dug up his body from its sepulchre among kings, hung it on a gallows, and shovelled the headless trunk into a felon's grave. But though they might tear out his laws from the statute-book and hide away his charters, there was one part of his life's work which they could not destroy. He found the English in the East struggling, humiliated, in despair. He left them with their future assured. He was the first ruler of England who realized that the India trade was no private preserve of the sovereign and his nominees, but a concern of the nation, to be maintained by national diplomacy and defended by the national arms. His union of conflicting Anglo-Indian interests in 1657 anticipated the great Parliamentary fusion of those interests fifty years later. Under his charter the East India Company transformed itself from a feeble relic of the mediæval trade-guild into the vigorous forerunner of the modern Joint Stock Company. A large and continuous capital, always capable of automatic increase, took the place of a successions of uncertain subscriptions, each of them intended to be dissolved at the end of a few years.

While Cromwell thus renewed the East India Company and placed it on its permanent basis at home, abroad he secured for England the recognition of her right to a free expansion in the East. The arrogant claims of the Catholic powers in Asia he blew from the cannon's mouth. Our great Protestant compeer had to learn that similarity in religion formed no excuse for commercial wrong-doing. Cromwell's sea-rivalry with Holland hardened and set into a national tradition, which dominated the feeling of the English trading classes for thirty years; and in the end led to the overthrow of the Dutch supremacy in Asia and to the establishment of our own. The head which planned these great designs was set to shrivel on a pole. But if the grandson of Cromwell's secretary, Milton, died as parish clerk in Madras, both the grandson and great-grandson of the Protector lived to be governors of Bengal.

APPENDIX II

STATISTICAL TABLES

A. The Fifteen Separate Voyages of the Dutch to the Indies, 1595–1601.

Number of Voyages	Names of Commanders	Names of the Separate Companies	Number of Vessels	Date of Departure	Date of Return
1	Houtman	Compagnie van Verre, Amsterdam	4	April 2, 1595	April 14, 1597
2	Jakob Corneliszoon van Neck	Oude Compagnie Amsterdam	8	May 1, 1598	July 19, 1599 May 19, 1600 Sept., 1600
3	Houtman	Moucheron, Veere	2	Mar. 15, 1598	July 29, 1600
4	Gerard Leroy and Laurens Bikker	Compagnie van Middelburg	3	1598	1600
5	Jacques Mahu and Simon de Cordes	J. van der Veken & Cie, Rotterdam	5	June 27, 1598	—
6	Olivier van Noort . .	Rotterdam	4	July 2, 1598	Aug. 12, 1601
7	Steven van der Hagen	Oude Compagnie, Amsterdam	3	April 26, 1599	July, 1601
8	Pieter Both van Amersfoort	Nieuwe Brabantsche Compagnie, Amsterdam	4	Dec. 21, 1599	1601
9	Jakob Wilkens . . .	Oude Compagnie, Amsterdam	4	Dec. 21, 1599	1601
10	Van Neck	Oude Compagnie, Amsterdam	6	June 28, 1600	July 15, 1602, 1603, 1604
11	Guljam Seneschal . .	Nieuwe Brabantsche Compagnie, Amsterdam	2	June 28, 1600	1601
12	Cornelis Bastiaanszoon	Compagnie van Middelburg	4	Jan. 28, 1601	July 6, 1602
13	Jakob van Heemskerck	Vereenigde Hollandsche Compagnie, Amsterdam	8	April 23, 1601	May, 1603, 1602, 1604
14	Wolphert Harmenszoon	Vereenigde Hollandsche Compagnie, Amsterdam	5	April 23, 1601	March, 1603
15	Joris Spilbergh . . .	Moucheron, Veere	3	May 5, 1601	1604
			65		

From *Les Premiers Voyages des Néerlandais dans l'Insulinde* (1595–1602) by Prince Roland Bonaparte (Versailles, 1884).

B. Ships Sent on the First Voyage of the English East India Company in 1601.

NAME OF SHIP	TONNAGE	NUMBER OF CREW	COMMANDER
The *Red Dragon* (formerly the *Mare Scurge*) . .	600 tons	202 men	James Lancaster, Admiral of the expedition
The *Hector* . .	300 "	108 "	John Middleton
The *Ascension* . .	260 "	82 "	William Brand
The *Susan* . .	240 "	88 "	John Heyward
Total . .	1400 tons	480 men	

C. **The First Nine Voyages of the East India Company: 1601–1612**

As shown in the India Office folio of "Marine Records" (Introd. p. ix.), with the profits added from Bruce's "Annals"

	Date of Voyage	Capital	Exported in Money	Exported in Goods	Cost of Ships and Victuals	Ships Sent out	Profits on the Venture
First . . .	1601	68,373	21,742	6,860	39,771	4	95 p. c.
Second . . .	1604	60,450	11,160	1,142	48,150	4	95 p. c.
Third . . .	1607	53,500	17,600	7,280	28,620	3	234 p. c.
Fourth . . .	1608	33,000	15,000	3,400	14,600	2	Both ships wrecked
Fifth . . .	1609	13,700	6,000	1,700	6,000	1	234 p. c.
Sixth . . .	1610	82,000	28,500	21,300	32,200	3	121⅔ p. c.
Seventh . . .	1611	71,581	19,200	10,081	42,500	4	218 p. c.
Eighth . . .	1612	76,375	17,675	10,000	48,700	4	211 p. c.
Ninth . . .	1612	7,200	1,250	650	5,300	1	160 p. c.
		466,179	138,127	62,413	265,841	26	

D. Marine Records of the Four Voyages of the First Joint Stock, 1613–1616.

Date of Voyage	Capital	Exported in Money	Exported in Goods	Cost of Ships and Victuals	Ships sent out
	£	£	£	£	
1613	106,000	18,810	12,446	272,544 (1613–1616)	5
1614	107,000	13,942	23,000		9
1615	107,000	26.660	26,065		8
1616	109,000	52,087	16,506		7
	429,000	111,499	78,017	272,544	29

INDEX

INDEX

C

E

N

O

P

Published by

Facsimile Publisher
Ashok Vihar, Delhi-110052 (India)
Website: www.facsimilepublisher.com

Distributed by

Gyan Books Pvt. Ltd.
5, Ansari Road, Daryaganj, New Delhi-110002 (India)
E-mail: books@gyanbooks.com, Website: www.gyanbooks.com

8 888000 714583